INSIDE

LANGUAGE · LITERACY · CONTENT

Acknowledgments

Grateful acknowledgment is given to the authors, artists, photographers, museums, publishers, and agents for permission to reprint copyrighted material. Every effort has been made to secure the appropriate permission. If any omissions have been made or if corrections are required, please contact the Publisher.

Photographic Credits

Cover (front): Leafcutter Bee on Fishhook Barrel Cactus Blossom, Sonoran Desert, Arizona, USA, John Cancalosi. Photograph © John Cancalosi/Peter Arnold/Getty Images.

Acknowledgments continue on page 191.

For product information and technology asistance, contact us at
Cengage Learning Customer & Sales Support, 1-800-354-9706

For permission to use material from this text or product, submit all requests online at **www.cengage.com/permissions**
Further permissions questions can be emailed to
permissionrequest@cengage.com

National Geographic Learning | Cengage Learning
1 Lower Ragsdale Drive
Building 1, Suite 200
Monterey, CA 93940

Cengage Learning is a leading provider of customized learning solutions with office locations around the globe, including Singapore, the United Kingdom, Australia, Mexico, Brazil, and Japan. Locate your local office at **www.cengage.com/global**.

Visit National Geographic Learning online at **ngl.cengage.com**
Visit our corporate website at **www.cengage.com**

ISBN: 978-12857-34712 (Practice Book)
ISBN: 978-12857-34668 (Practice Book Teacher's Annotated Edition)

ISBN: 978-12857-67963 (Practice Masters)
Teachers are authorized to reproduce the practice masters in this book in limited quantity and solely for use in their own classrooms.

Printed in the United States of America
Print Number: 17   Print Year: 2024

INSIDE

LANGUAGE · LITERACY · CONTENT

NATIONAL GEOGRAPHIC LEARNING | CENGAGE Learning®

Contents

Foundations of Reading

Unit 1

Unit 2

Contents, continued

Foundations of Reading

Name _____

▶ Letters and Sounds

A. Study the new letters and sounds.

Ss   **Mm**   **Ff**   **Hh**   **Tt**   **Aa**

B. Say the name of each picture below. What letter spells the <u>first</u> sound you hear? Circle the letter.

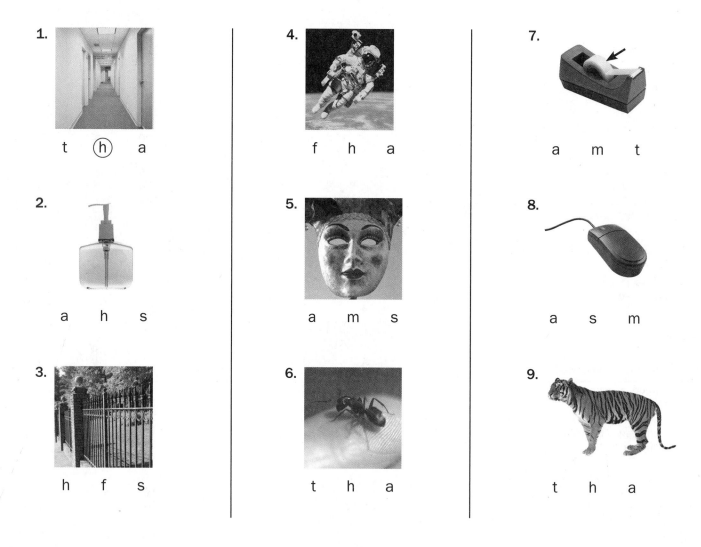

1.

   t   (h)   a

2.

   a   h   s

3.

   h   f   s

4.

   f   h   a

5.

   a   m   s

6.

   t   h   a

7.

   a   m   t

8.

   a   s   m

9.

   t   h   a

Foundations of Reading

▶ **Letters and Sounds**

Say the name of each picture below. What letter spells the <u>first</u> sound you hear? Write the letter.

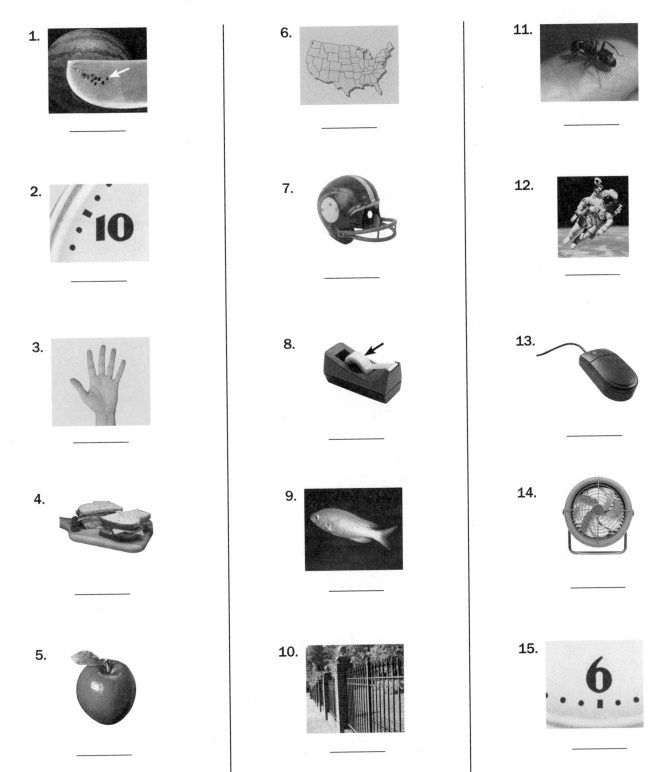

1. _____

2. _____

3. _____

4. _____

5. _____

6. _____

7. _____

8. _____

9. _____

10. _____

11. _____

12. _____

13. _____

14. _____

15. _____

Foundations of Reading

▶ High Frequency Words

Read each word. Then write it.

1. am _____ 4. school _____

2. I _____ 5. the _____

3. is _____ 6. this _____

How to Play

1. Make a spinner.

2. Write the name of each player on a blank.

3. Spin. Read the sentence.

The first player to read all six sentences wins.

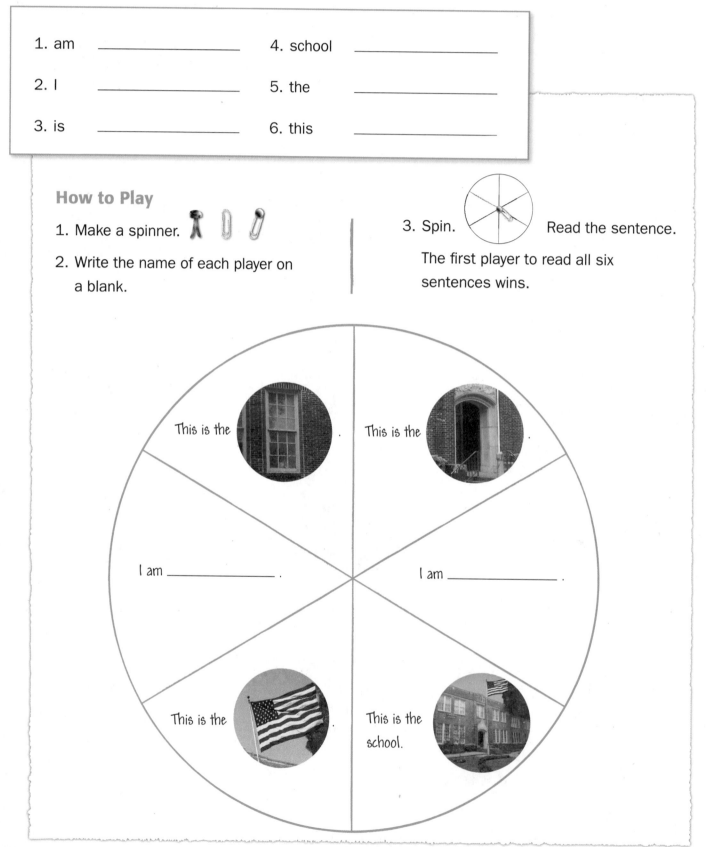

This is the ____ .

This is the ____ .

I am _____ .

I am _____ .

This is the ____ .

This is the school.

Foundations of Reading

Name _____

► High Frequency Words

Read each word. Then write it.

1. a _____	4. my _____
2. an _____	5. no _____
3. here _____	6. you _____

---

1. Find the words. Circle them.
Look across. →

q	ⓐ	o	p	t	m
v	l	e	s	a	n
s	b	m	l	n	l
h	e	r	e	o	r
z	p	l	g	m	y
n	o	r	z	q	w
w	f	y	o	u	z
x	g	q	t	d	s

5. Find the words. Circle them.
Look down. ↓

a	q	h	j	z	t
n	v	e	u	n	s
k	s	r	r	o	g
l	b	e	h	o	y
r	a	i	z	e	o
x	f	s	m	r	u
w	g	o	y	e	q
p	u	z	e	l	v

Write the missing words.

2. Here is ___my___ 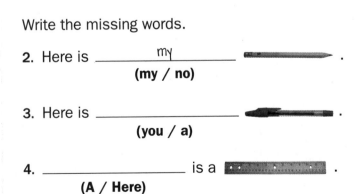 .
   (my / no)

3. Here is _____ .
   (you / a)

4. _____ is a .
   (A / Here)

Write the missing words.

6. This is ___an___ 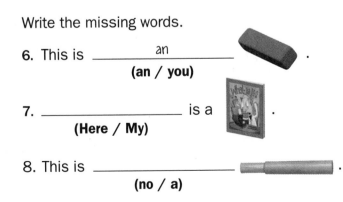 .
   (an / you)

7. _____ is a .
   (Here / My)

8. This is _____ .
   (no / a)

Foundations of Reading

Name _____

► High Frequency Words

A. Read each word. Then write it.

1. at	_____	4. of	_____
2. it	_____	5. on	_____
3. look	_____	6. yes	_____

B. Write the missing letters.

7. Which words have a **t**?

<u>a</u> <u>t</u> ____ ____

8. Which words have 2 letters?

____ ____   ____ ____

____ ____   ____ ____

9. Which word has 3 letters?

____ ____ ____

10. Which word has 4 letters?

____ ____ ____ ____

11. Which words start with **o**?

____ ____   ____ ____

12. Which word has an **f**?

____ ____

C. Write the missing words.

13. Carlos, _____ at this!
    (of / look)

14. Is this the school?

    Yes, _____ is.
    (it / at)

15. I am _____ school.
    (at / of)

16. This is a [image] _____

    the school.   **(of / look)**

17. The [image] is _____

    the [image] .   **(it / on)**

▶ **Read on Your Own**

Read these sentences.

Sam has ham.

_____

Sam has a hat.

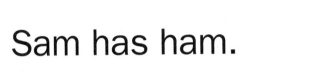

_____

Sam has a mat.

Foundations of Reading

▶ Words with Short *a*

A. Read each word. Draw a line to match the word and the picture.

1.

hat

ham

2.

fat

mat

B. Write the missing words.

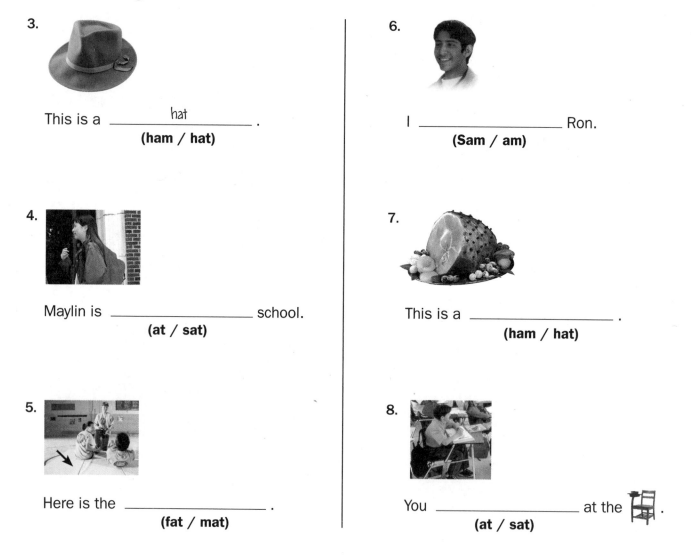

3.

This is a _____hat_____ .
(ham / hat)

4.

Maylin is _____ school.
(at / sat)

5.

Here is the _____ .
(fat / mat)

6.

I _____ Ron.
(Sam / am)

7.

This is a _____ .
(ham / hat)

8.

You _____ at the 🪑 .
(at / sat)

► Words with Short *a*

A. Write the missing *a*. Then read the words in each list. How are the words different?

1.

<u>a</u> m

S ___ m

h ___ m

2.

___ t

h ___ t

s ___ t

3.

___ t

f ___ t

m ___ t

B. What word completes each sentence and tells about the picture? Spell the word.

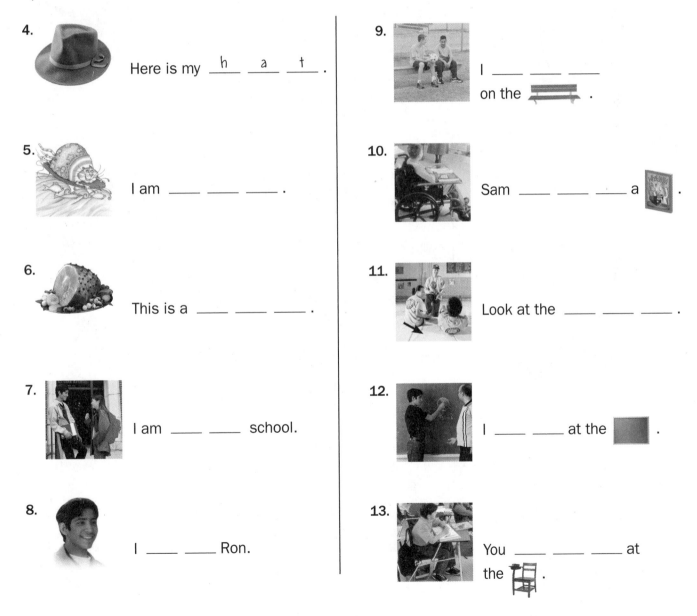

4.

Here is my __h__ __a__ __t__ .

5.

I am ___ ___ ___ .

6.

This is a ___ ___ ___ .

7.

I am ___ ___ school.

8.

I ___ ___ Ron.

9.

I ___ ___ ___ on the ___ .

10.

Sam ___ ___ ___ a ___ .

11.

Look at the ___ ___ ___ .

12.

I ___ ___ at the ___ .

13.

You ___ ___ ___ at the ___ .

Foundations of Reading

▶ Letters and Sounds

A. Study the new letters and sounds.

Nn	Ll	Pp	Gg	Ii

B. Say the name of each picture below. What letter spells the <u>first</u> sound you hear? Circle the letter.

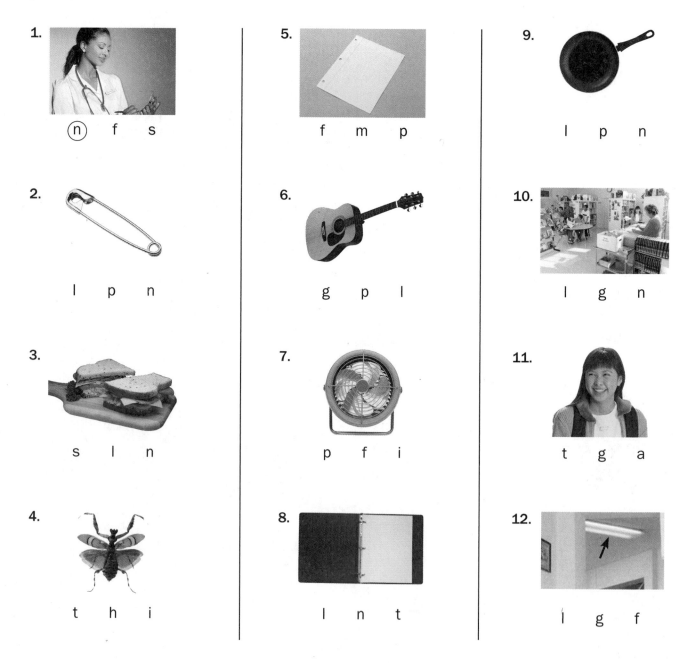

1. (n) f s

2. l p n

3. s l n

4. t h i

5. f m p

6. g p l

7. p f i

8. l n t

9. l p n

10. l g n

11. t g a

12. l g f

Foundations of Reading

▶ **Letters and Sounds**

Say the name of each picture below. Write the missing letters.

1.
h   a   m

2.
___ ___ ___

3.
___ i ___

4.
s ___ i ___

5.
___ i ___

6.
m ___ ___

7.
___ ___ ___

8.
___ ___ m p

9.
___ ___ ___

10.
m ___ ___

11.
___ i ___

12.
___ ___ ___

Foundations of Reading

Name _____

▶ High Frequency Words

A. Read each word. Then write it.

1. are	_____	4. show	_____
2. good	_____	5. where	_____
3. see	_____	6. he	_____

B. Write the missing letters.

7. Which words have 4 letters?

<u>g</u>   <u>o</u>   <u>o</u>   <u>d</u>

____ ____ ____ ____

8. Which word has an **a**?

____ ____ ____

9. Which word has 5 letters?

____ ____ ____ ____ ____

10. Which words have 3 letters?

____ ____ ____

____ ____ ____

11. Which word has a **g**?

____ ____ ____ ____

12. Which words have a **w**?

____ ____ ____ ____ ____

____ ____ ____ ____

13. Which word has 2 letters?

____ ____

C. Write the missing word.

14. I _____ two pens.
       (see / are)

15. Where _____ the people?
          (are / he)

16. This is a _____ sandwich.
          (good / see)

17. _____ me the motorcycle.
  (Show / Where)

18. _____ is the boy?
  (Show / Where)

19. We do not know who _____
is.   **(see / he)**

▶ **High Frequency Words**

A. Read each word. Then write it.

1. answer _____   4. time _____

2. she _____   5. who _____

3. some _____   6. your _____

B. Write the missing letters.

7. Which word has 6 letters?

<u>a</u> <u>n</u> <u>s</u> <u>w</u> <u>e</u> <u>r</u>

8. Which words have an **m**?

____ ____ ____ ____

____ ____ ____ ____

9. Which words have 3 letters?

____ ____ ____

____ ____

10. Which words have 4 letters?

____ ____ ____ ____

____ ____ ____ ____

____ ____ ____ ____

11. Which words have a **w**?

____ ____ ____ ____ ____

____ ____ ____

12. Which word has a **y**?

____ ____ ____ ____

C. Write the missing word.

13. I write the _____ .
        (answer / some)

14. _____ is my friend.
    (She / Your)

15. What _____ is class?
        (time / your)

16. _____ puppy is very cute.
    (Your / Who)

17. I have _____ homework.
        (some / who)

18. _____ do you see?
    (Who / She)

▶ **High Frequency Words**

A. Read each word. Then write it.

1. point _____
2. read _____
3. to _____
4. with _____
5. work _____
6. write _____

B. Write the missing letters.

7. Which words have 4 letters?

___ ___ ___ ___

___ ___ ___ ___

___ ___ ___ ___

8. Which words have a **w**?

___ ___ ___ ___

___ ___ ___ ___

___ ___ ___ ___ ___

9. Which words have 5 letters?

___ ___ ___ ___ ___

___ ___ ___ ___ ___

10. Which word has a **k**?

___ ___ ___ ___

11. Which words have an **r**?

___ ___ ___ ___

___ ___ ___ ___

___ ___ ___ ___

C. Write the missing word.

12. I _____ a book.
    (read / point)

13. I _____ to the answer.
    (work / point)

14. Carlos will _____ on
    (write / with)
    the board.

15. I need _____ see you.
    (point / to)

16. I will go _____ Lisa to
    (with / read)
    the store.

17. Eli likes to _____ on
    (with / work)
    computers.

► **Read on Your Own**

Read these sentences.

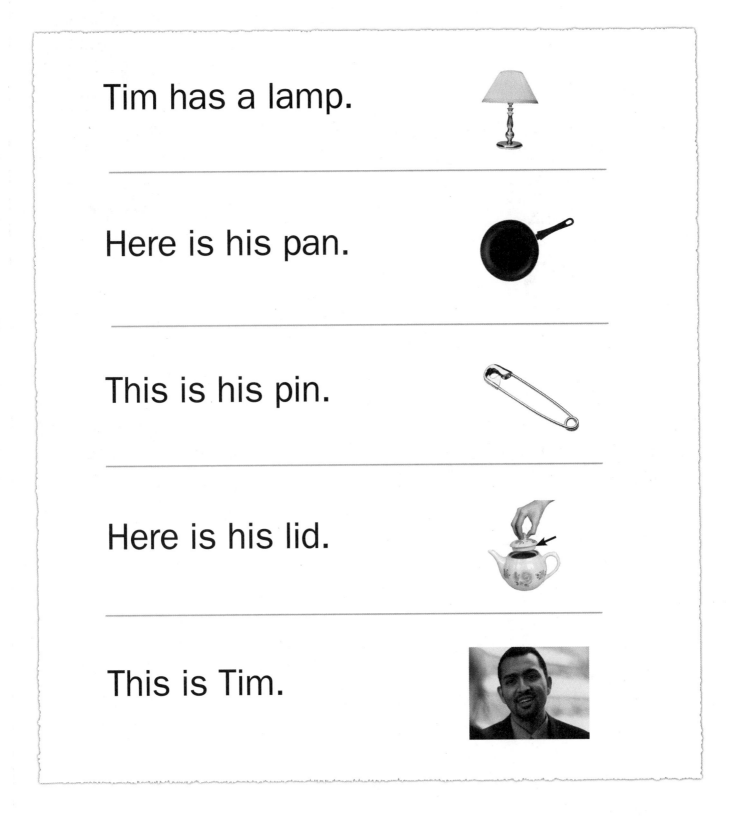

Tim has a lamp.

Here is his pan.

This is his pin.

Here is his lid.

This is Tim.

Foundations of Reading

Name _____

▶ **Words with Short *a* and *i***

A. Read each word. Draw a line to match the word and the picture.

1.

pan

map

man

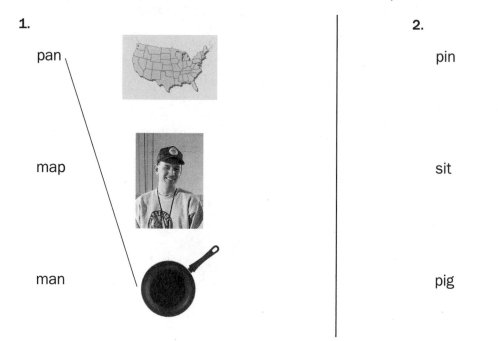

2.

pin

sit

pig

B. Write the missing words.

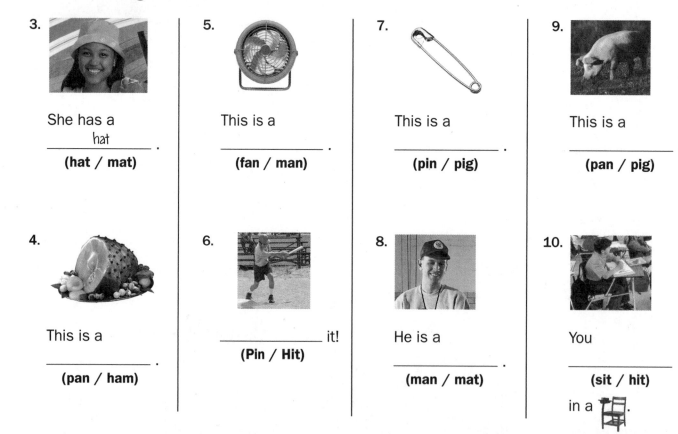

3.

She has a
_____hat_____ .
(hat / mat)

5.

This is a
_____ .
(fan / man)

7.

This is a
_____ .
(pin / pig)

9.

This is a
_____ .
(pan / pig)

4.

This is a
_____ .
(pan / ham)

6.

_____ it!
(Pin / Hit)

8.

He is a
_____ .
(man / mat)

10.

You
_____
(sit / hit)
in a 🪑.

Foundations of Reading

► Words with Short *a* and *i*

A. Write the missing letters. Then read the words in each list. How are the words different?

1.
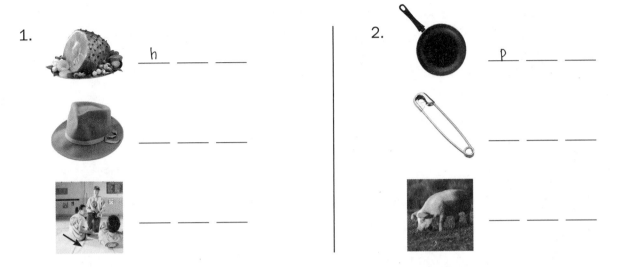

h ___ ___

___ ___ ___

___ ___ ___

2.

p ___ ___

___ ___ ___

___ ___ ___

B. Read each question. What word goes in the answer? Spell the word.
Then circle the correct picture.

3. Where is the pig?

The __p__ __i__ __g__ is here.

4. Where is the pan?

Here is the ___ ___ ___ .

5. Where is Sam?

___ ___ ___ is here.

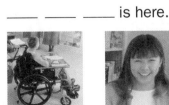

6. Who hit it?

Carlos ___ ___ ___ it.

7. Who has the hat?

She ___ ___ ___ the hat.

8. Who is the man?

He is the ___ ___ ___ .

▶ Letters and Sounds

A. Study the new letters and sounds.

Rr   **Dd**   **Cc**   **Vv**   **Oo**

B. Say the name of each picture below. What letter spells the <u>first</u> sound you hear? Circle the letter.

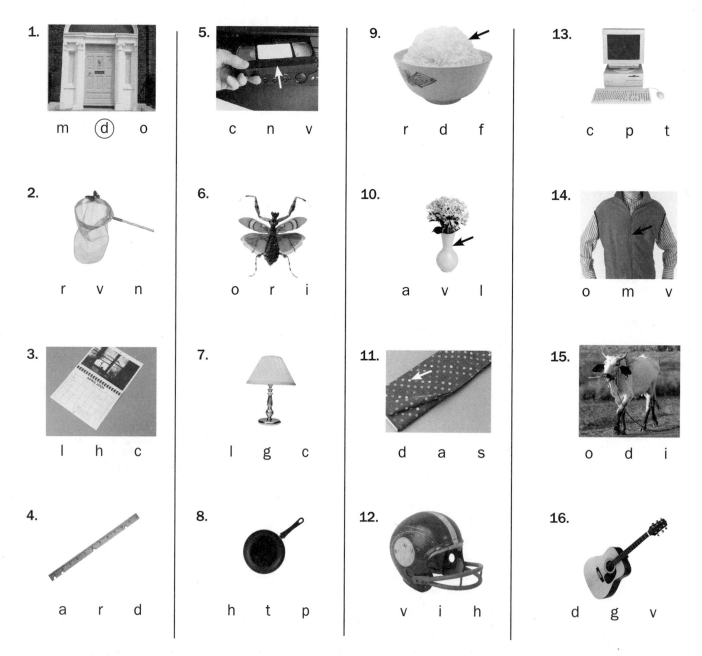

1.   m   (d)   o

2.   r   v   n

3.   l   h   c

4.   a   r   d

5.   c   n   v

6.   o   r   i

7.   l   g   c

8.   h   t   p

9.   r   d   f

10.   a   v   l

11.   d   a   s

12.   v   i   h

13.   c   p   t

14.   o   m   v

15.   o   d   i

16.   d   g   v

Foundations of Reading

▶ **Letters and Sounds**

Say the name of each picture below. Write the missing letters.

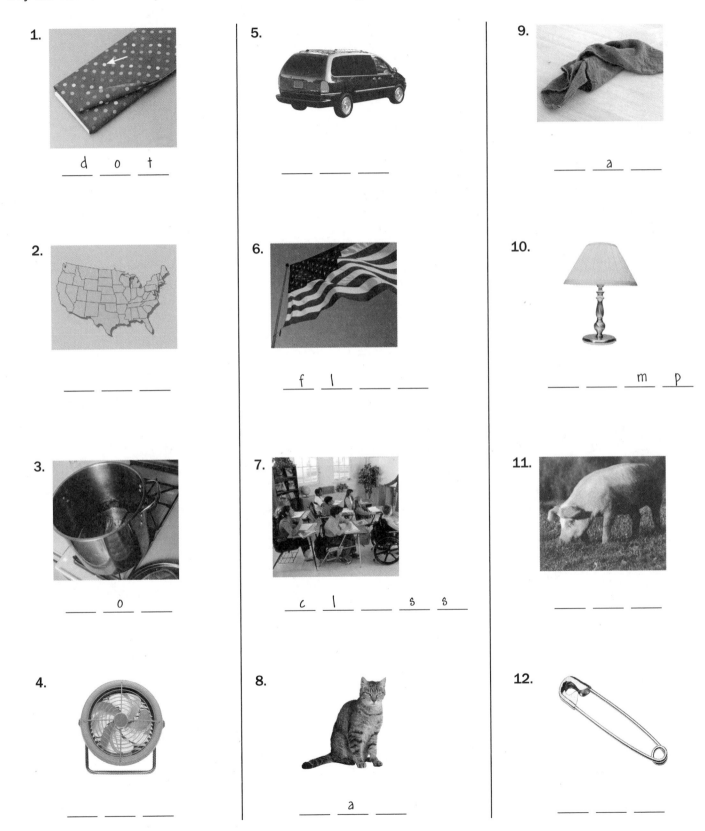

1. d o t

2. ___ ___ ___

3. ___ o ___

4. ___ ___ ___

5. ___ ___ ___

6. f l ___ ___

7. c l ___ s s

8. ___ a ___

9. ___ a ___ ___

10. ___ ___ m p

11. ___ ___ ___

12. ___ ___ ___

▶ High Frequency Words

Read each word. Then write it.

1. do	_____	4. help	_____
2. does	_____	5. in	_____
3. for	_____	6. like	_____

How to Play

1. Play with a partner. Each partner chooses a sign. **X O**

2. Partner 1 reads a word and marks the square with a sign.

3. Partner 2 takes a turn.

4. Get 3 **X**s or **O**s in a row to win.

A.

do	help	like
in	does	for
point	read	to

B.

does	point	read
in	do	help
for	like	to

C.

help	does	do
for	like	in
with	work	write

D.

like	work	does
write	do	help
for	with	in

▶ High Frequency Words

A. Read each word. Then write it.

1. around _____   4. will _____

2. me _____   5. and _____

3. picture _____   6. don't _____

B. Write the missing letters.

7. Which word has 3 letters?

   _a_ _n_ _d_

8. Which word is two words together?

   ___ ___ ___ ___

9. Which word has 6 letters?

   ___ ___ ___ ___ ___ ___

10. Which words have an **r**?

    ___ ___ ___ ___ ___ ___

    ___ ___ ___ ___ ___ ___ ___

11. Which word has 2 letters?

    ___ ___

12. Which words have a **d**?

    ___ ___ ___ ___ ___ ___ ___

    ___ ___ ___

    ___ ___ ___ ___

C. Write the missing word.

13. I see your _____ in
    (picture / around)
    the yearbook.

14. Yes, I _____
    (don't / will)
    play basketball.

15. Tell _____ about
    (and / me)
    the game.

16. Can you run _____
    (around / picture)
    the track?

17. Why _____ you
    (don't / and)
    stay there?

Foundations of Reading

► **High Frequency Words**

A. Read each word. Then write it.

1. food _____	4. both _____
2. not _____	5. get _____
3. that _____	6. these _____

B. Write the missing letters.

7. Which words have 3 letters?

    _n_   _o_   _t_

    _g_   _e_   _t_

8. Which words have 4 letters?

    ___ ___ ___ ___

    ___ ___ ___ ___

    ___ ___ ___ ___

9. Which words end in **t**?

    ___ ___ ___

    ___ ___ ___

    ___ ___ ___ ___

10. Which words have an **e**?

    ___ ___ ___

    ___ ___ ___ ___ ___

11. Which word has 5 letters?

    ___ ___ ___ ___ ___

C. Write the missing word.

12. I ate the _____ .
                  (both / food)

13. Sam saw _____ apple.
                  (get / that)

14. I did _____ see the
              (get / not)
shooting star.

15. Did you _____ help
                (both / food)
the girl?

16. Did Lin _____ the ball?
               (these / get)

17. We ate _____ chips.
               (food / these)

▶ **Read on Your Own**

Read these sentences.

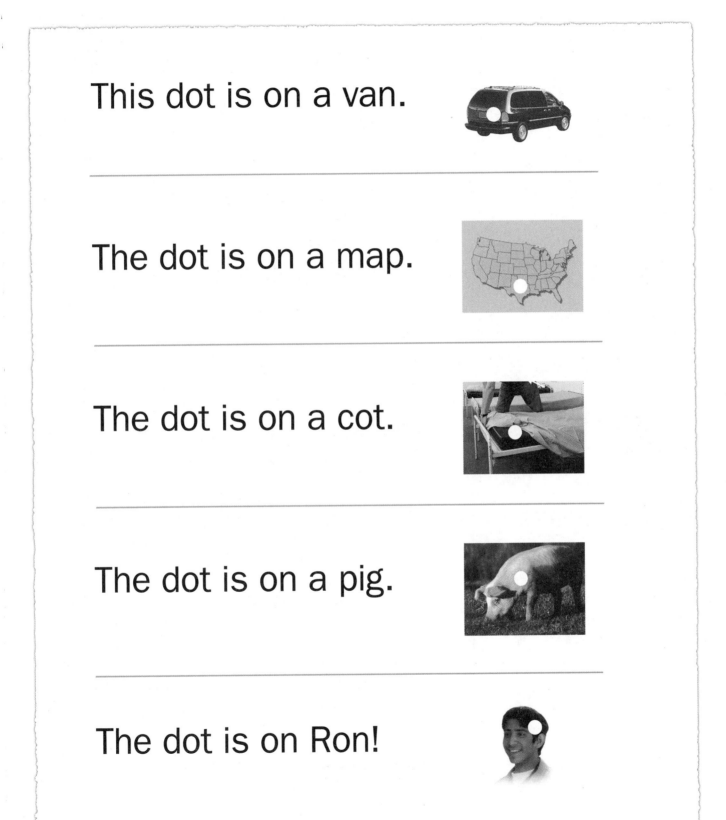

This dot is on a van.

The dot is on a map.

The dot is on a cot.

The dot is on a pig.

The dot is on Ron!

Name _____

▶ Words with Short *a*, *i*, and *o*

A. Read each word. Draw a line to the correct picture.

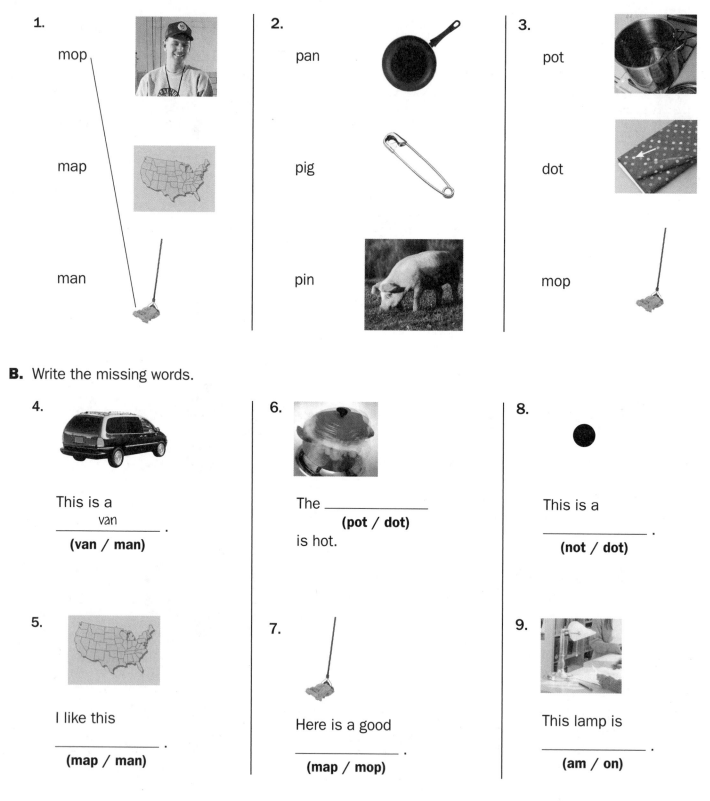

1.

mop

map

man

2.

pan

pig

pin

3.

pot

dot

mop

B. Write the missing words.

4.

This is a
___van___ .
(van / man)

6.

The _____
(pot / dot)
is hot.

8.

This is a
_____ .
(not / dot)

5.

I like this
_____ .
(map / man)

7.

Here is a good
_____ .
(map / mop)

9.

This lamp is
_____ .
(am / on)

Name _____

▶ Words with Short *a*, *i*, and *o*

A. Write the missing letters. Then read the words in each list. How are the words different?

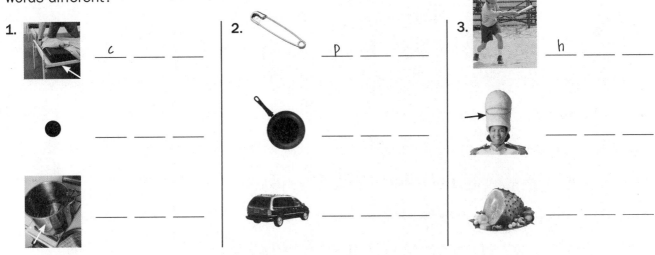

1. c ___ ___

   ___ ___ ___

   ___ ___ ___

2. p ___ ___

   ___ ___ ___

   ___ ___ ___

3. h ___ ___

   ___ ___ ___

   ___ ___ ___

B. Read each question and the answer. Write the missing words. Then circle the correct picture.

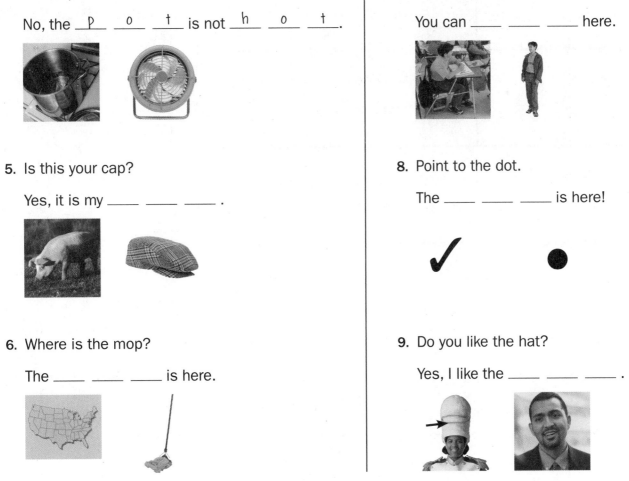

4. Is this pot hot?

   No, the p o t is not h o t .

5. Is this your cap?

   Yes, it is my ___ ___ ___ .

6. Where is the mop?

   The ___ ___ ___ is here.

7. Where can I sit?

   You can ___ ___ ___ here.

8. Point to the dot.

   The ___ ___ ___ is here!

9. Do you like the hat?

   Yes, I like the ___ ___ ___ .

Foundations of Reading

► Letters and Sounds

Study the new letters and sounds.

Jj　　　**Bb**　　　**Ww**　　　**Kk**　　　**Ee**

How to Play Bingo

1. Write the letters from the box. Write one letter in each square.

2. Then listen to the word your teacher reads.

3. Put a ◯ on the letter that stands for the first sound in the word.

4. The first player to cover all the letters in a row is the winner.

Letters to Write

a	i	p
b	j	r
b	j	s
c	k	t
d	k	v
e	l	w
f	m	w
g	n	
h	o	

Words to Read

am	got	lot	top
bat	hit	mat	van
big	it	not	win
can	jam	on	wig
dot	jog	pin	
egg	kid	red	
fat	kit	sit	

Foundations of Reading

Name _____

► **Letters and Sounds**

Say the name of each picture below. Write the missing letters.

1.

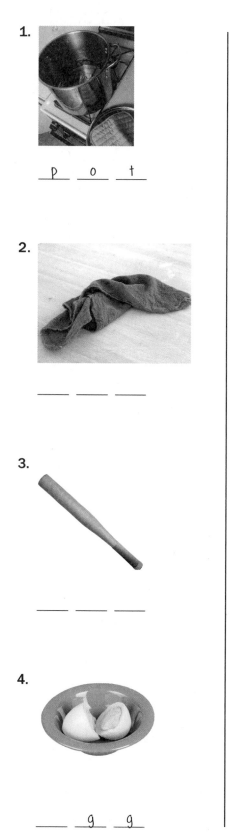

p   o   t

2.

___ ___ ___

3.

___ ___ ___

4.

___ g   g

5.

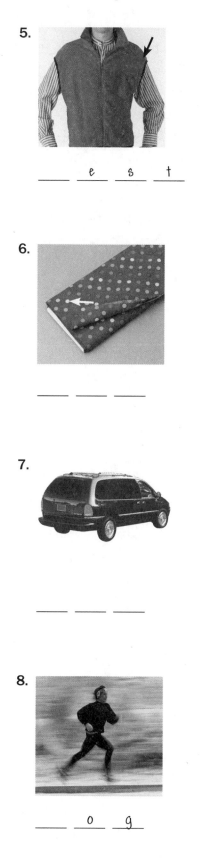

___ e   s   t

6.

___ ___ ___

7.

___ ___ ___

8.

___ o   g

9.

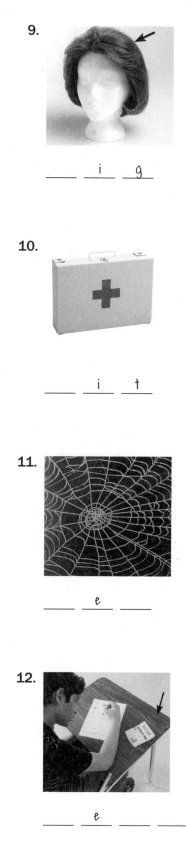

___ i   g

10.

___ i   t

11.

___ e   ___ ___

12.

___ e   ___ ___

Foundations of Reading

► High Frequency Words

A. Read each word. Then write it.

1. things   _____
2. little   _____
3. old   _____
4. them   _____
5. those   _____
6. very   _____

B. Write the missing letters.

7. Which word has 3 letters?

   <u>o</u>   <u>l</u>   <u>d</u>

8. Which words have an **i**?

   ___ ___ ___ ___ ___ ___

   ___ ___ ___ ___ ___ ___

9. Which word has a **v**?

   ___ ___ ___ ___

10. Which words have 4 letters?

    ___ ___ ___ ___

    ___ ___ ___ ___

C. Write the missing word.

11. The food is _____ good.
    (very / little)

12. Did you see _____
    (things / those)
    bananas?

13. The flea was very _____ .
    (them / little)

14. I saw _____ at school.
    (them / very)

15. The _____ dog liked
    (things / old)
    to sleep.

16. I have many _____ .
    (those / things)

Name _____

► High Frequency Words

A. Read each word. Then write it.

1. think	_____	4. which	_____
2. take	_____	5. can	_____
3. give	_____	6. play	_____

B. Write the missing letters.

7. Which words have 4 letters?

<u>t</u> <u>a</u> <u>k</u> <u>e</u>

___ ___ ___ ___

___ ___ ___ ___

8. Which words have 5 letters?

___ ___ ___ ___ ___

___ ___ ___ ___ ___

9. Which word has a **g**?

___ ___ ___ ___

10. Which word has 3 letters?

___ ___ ___

11. Which words have an **a**?

___ ___ ___

___ ___ ___ ___

___ ___ ___ ___

C. Write the missing word.

12. I _____ I know the
    (think / play)
    answer.

13. Juan _____ run very fast.
    (which / can)

14. _____ your turn next.
    (Take / Which)

15. Can you _____ baseball?
    (can / play)

16. _____ book is yours?
    (Take / Which)

17. Let's _____ food to the
    (give / play)
    hamster.

Foundations of Reading

Name _____

▶ High Frequency Words

A. Read each word. Then write it.

1. too _____   4. have _____

2. feel _____   5. how _____

3. has _____   6. put _____

B. Write the missing letters.

7. Which words have 3 letters?

__t__ __o__ __o__

____ ____ ____

____ ____ ____

____ ____ ____

8. Which words have 4 letters?

____ ____ ____ ____

____ ____ ____ ____

9. Which words have an **h**?

____ ____ ____

____ ____ ____

____ ____ ____ ____

10. Which word ends with a **t**?

____ ____ ____

11. Which word has two **e**'s?

____ ____ ____ ____

C. Write the missing word.

12. She has brown hair, _____ .
    (too / how)

13. Where did you _____
    (how / put)
    the book?

14. Do you _____ sick today?
    (have / feel)

15. She _____ a blue
    (has / have)
    backpack.

16. _____ are you feeling
    (Have / How)
    today?

17. I _____ two cookies.
    (how / have)

Name _____

▶ **Read on Your Own**

Read these sentences.

Can Ken jog?

Ken can jog well.

Can Ken get his bat?

Ken can get his bat.

Can Ken rest?

No. Ken has no bed!

Foundations of Reading

Name _____

► Words with Short *a*, *i*, *o*, and *e*

A. Read each word. Draw a line to the correct picture.

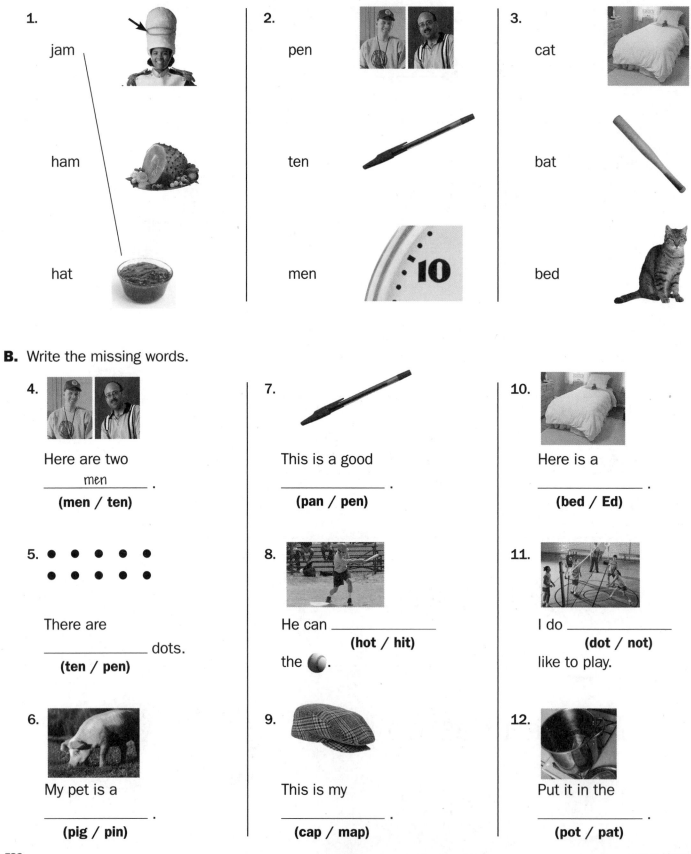

1.

jam

ham

hat

2.

pen

ten

men

3.

cat

bat

bed

B. Write the missing words.

4.

Here are two

___men___ .

(men / ten)

5.

There are

_____ dots.

(ten / pen)

6.

My pet is a

_____ .

(pig / pin)

7.

This is a good

_____ .

(pan / pen)

8.

He can _____

(hot / hit)

the ⬤ .

9.

This is my

_____ .

(cap / map)

10.

Here is a

_____ .

(bed / Ed)

11.

I do _____

(dot / not)

like to play.

12.

Put it in the

_____ .

(pot / pat)

F32

© NGSP & HB

Foundations of Reading

▶ Words with Short *a*, *i*, *o*, and *e*

A. Write the missing letters. Then read the words in each list. How are the words different?

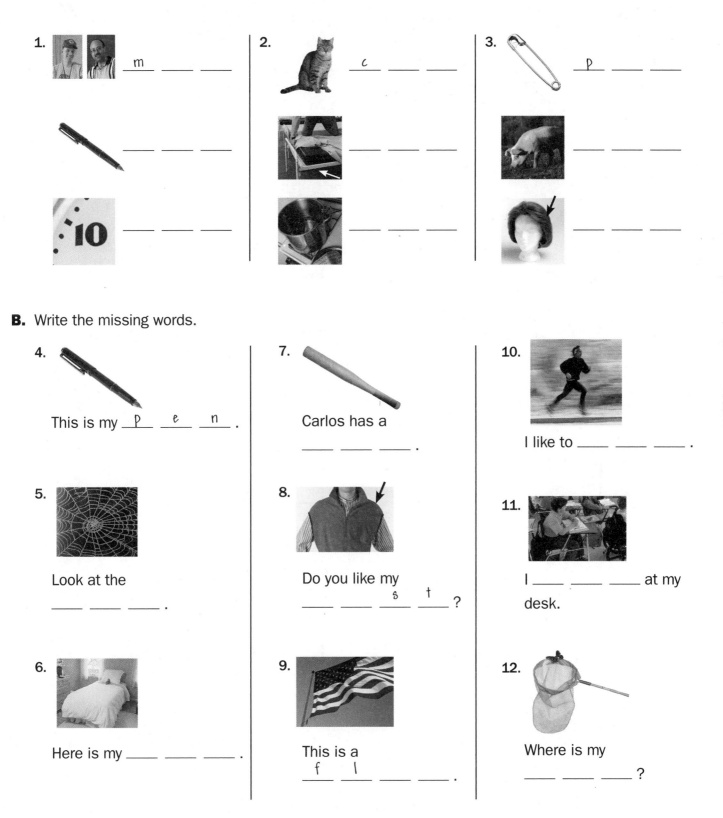

1. m __ __ __

   __ __ __

   __ __ __

2. c __ __ __

   __ __ __

   __ __ __

3. p __ __ __

   __ __ __

   __ __ __

B. Write the missing words.

4. This is my p e n .

5. Look at the __ __ __ .

6. Here is my __ __ __ .

7. Carlos has a __ __ __ .

8. Do you like my __ __ s t __ ?

9. This is a f l __ __ .

10. I like to __ __ __ .

11. I __ __ __ at my desk.

12. Where is my __ __ __ ?

Foundations of Reading

Name _____

▶ Letters and Sounds

Study the new letters and sounds.

Zz   **Yy**   **Uu**   **Qq**   **Xx**

How to Play Bingo

1. Write the letters from the box. Write one letter in each square.

2. Then listen to the word your teacher reads.

3. Put a ◯ on the letter that stands for the first sound in the word.

4. The first player to cover all the letters in a row is the winner.

Letters to Write

a	j	s
b	k	t
c	l	u
d	m	v
e	n	w
f	o	y
g	p	z
h	q	
i	r	

Words to Read

am	him	on	van
bat	in	pen	wig
cot	jam	quit	yes
dot	kid	red	zip
egg	lot	sat	
fan	map	ten	
got	not	up	

Foundations of Reading

Name _____

▶ Letters and Sounds

Say the name of each picture below. Write the missing letters.

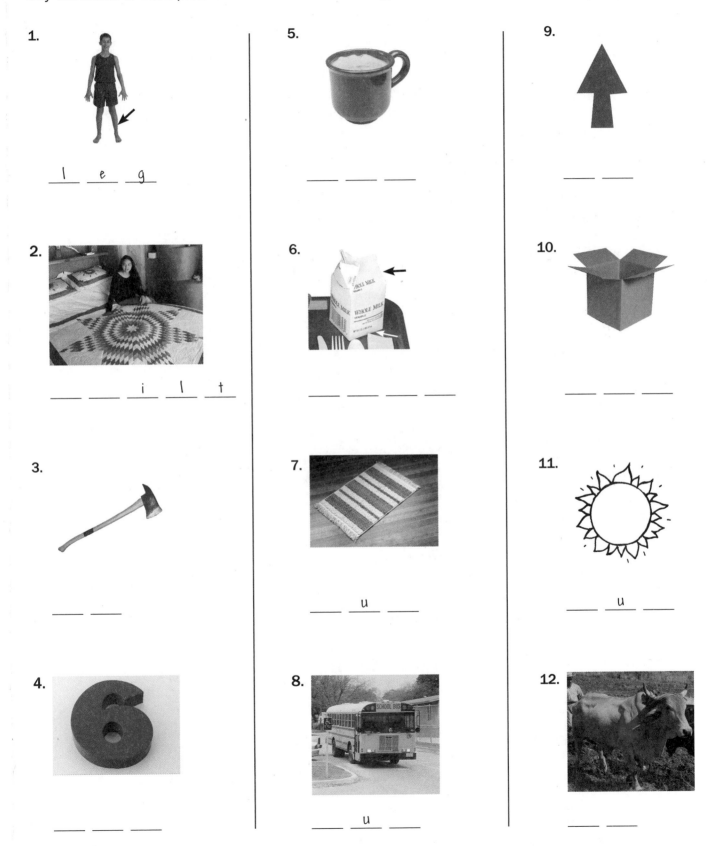

1.

$\underline{l} \quad \underline{e} \quad \underline{g}$

2.

___ ___ $\underline{i} \quad \underline{l} \quad \underline{t}$

3.

___ ___

4.

___ ___

5.

___ ___

6.

___ ___ ___

7.

___ $\underline{u}$ ___

8.

___ $\underline{u}$ ___

9.

___ ___

10.

___ ___ ___

11.

___ $\underline{u}$ ___

12.

___ ___

© NGSP & HB

F35

Foundations of Reading

Name _____

▶ High Frequency Words

A. Read each word. Then write it.

1. they   _____   4. soon   _____

2. great   _____   5. tomorrow _____

3. later   _____   6. call   _____

B. Write the missing letters.

7. Which words have 4 letters?

 t   h   e   y
___ ___ ___ ___

___ ___ ___ ___

___ ___ ___

8. Which words have 5 letters?

___ ___ ___ ___ ___

___ ___ ___ ___ ___

9. Which words have an **a**?

___ ___ ___ ___ ___

___ ___ ___ ___ ___

___ ___ ___ ___

10. Which word ends with a **t**?

___ ___ ___ ___

11. Which word has 8 letters?

___ ___ ___ ___ ___ ___ ___ ___

C. Write the missing word.

12. I will be in class _____ .
    (great / tomorrow)

13. I will see him _____ ,
    (soon / they)
    I hope!

14. Shana will be there _____ .
    (later / call)

15. Did you _____ your
    (call / soon)
    dad yet?

16. He did _____ on the test.
    (soon / great)

17. When will _____ be here?
    (they / call)

Foundations of Reading

► **High Frequency Words**

A. Read each word. Then write it.

1. name _____
2. need _____
3. number _____

4. we _____
5. what _____
6. book _____

B. Write the missing letters.

7. Which word has 2 letters?

__w__ __e__

8. Which words have 4 letters?

___ ___ ___ ___

___ ___ ___ ___

___ ___ ___ ___

___ ___ ___ ___

9. Which word has 6 letters?

___ ___ ___ ___ ___ ___

10. Which word ends with a **t**?

___ ___ ___ ___

11. Which word has an **r**?

___ ___ ___ ___ ___ ___

C. Write the missing word.

12. What is your _____ ?
    (we / name)

13. Find the _____ ten.
    (number / book)

14. The _____ is on the shelf.
    (book / need)

15. _____ went to the library.
    (We / Number)

16. I _____ to do my
    (need / what)
    homework.

17. _____ did you do last
    (What / We)
    week?

Foundations of Reading

▶ **High Frequency Words**

A. Read each word. Then write it.

1. boy	_____	4. group	_____
2. day	_____	5. letters	_____
3. girl	_____	6. night	_____
		7. year	_____

B. Write the missing letters.

8. Which word ends with a **p**?

   g____ r____ o____ u____ p____

9. Which words have 3 letters?

   ____ ____ ____

   ____ ____ ____

10. Which words have 5 letters?

   ____ ____ ____ ____ ____

   ____ ____ ____ ____ ____

11. Which word ends with **s**?

   ____ ____ ____ ____ ____ ____ ____

12. Which words have a **y** in them?

   ____ ____ ____ ____

   ____ ____ ____ ____

   ____ ____ ____

C. Write the missing word.

13. I saw the _____ in class.
    (night / boy)

14. Last _____, the sky
    (group / night)
    was clear.

15. He has many _____
    (letters / day)
    from Tom.

16. During the _____ the sun
    (day / night)
    is out.

17. The _____ plays basketball.
    (year / girl)

18. There is a _____
    (boy / group)
    of students.

19. This _____ I am a freshman.
    (night / year)

Name _____

▶ Read on Your Own

Read these sentences.

My quilt is big.

My rug is not big.

This ox is big.

This pup is not big.

That bus is very big!

That ant is not very big!

Foundations of Reading

Name _____

► Words with Short *a*, *i*, *o*, *e*, and *u*

A. Read each word. Draw a line to the correct picture.

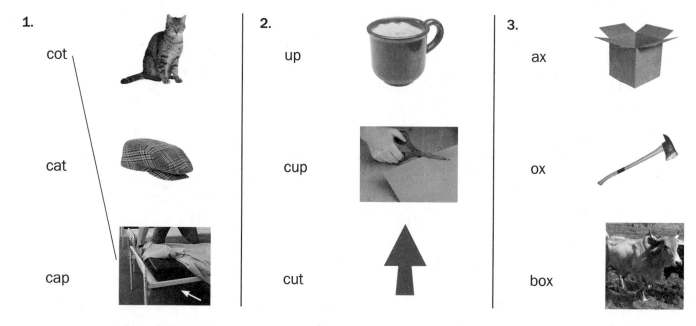

1.

cot

cat

cap

2.

up

cup

cut

3.

ax

ox

box

B. Say the name of each picture below. Write the missing letters.

4.

I can __z__ __i__ __p__ it.

6.

I like this old

___ ___ ___ ___ ___ .

8.

I have ___ ___ ___

pins.

5.

This is my ___ ___ ___ .

7.

Do you like my little

___ ___ ___ ?

9.

Is this a pig?

___ ___ ___ !

Foundations of Reading

► Words with Short *a, i, o, e,* and *u*

A. Write the missing letters. Then read the words in each list. How are the words different?

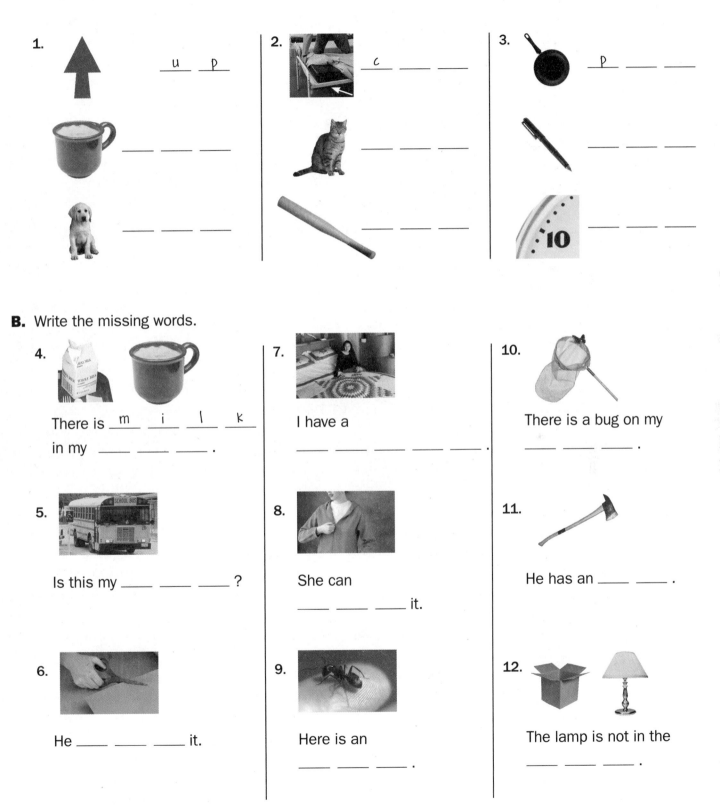

1. __u__ __p__

___ ___ ___

___ ___ ___

2. __c__ ___ ___

___ ___ ___

___ ___ ___

3. __p__ ___ ___

___ ___ ___

___ ___ ___

B. Write the missing words.

4. There is __m__ __i__ __l__ __k__ in my ___ ___ ___ .

5. Is this my ___ ___ ___ ?

6. He ___ ___ ___ it.

7. I have a ___ ___ ___ ___ ___ .

8. She can ___ ___ ___ it.

9. Here is an ___ ___ ___ .

10. There is a bug on my ___ ___ ___ .

11. He has an ___ ___ .

12. The lamp is not in the ___ ___ ___ .

Mind Map

Use the mind map to show what personal information is and how to share it.
As you read the selections in this unit, add new ideas you learn about getting
to know people.

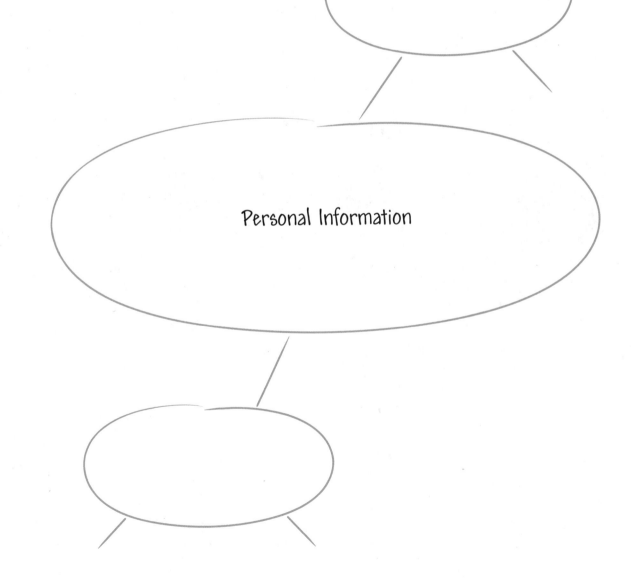

Personal Information

Language Development

Use Pronouns in Greetings

▶ **Language: Exchange Greetings and Good-byes**

▶ **Grammar: Pronouns**

A. Study the chart.

Greetings and Good-byes

Greetings	Questions and Answers	Good-byes
Hi!	How are you?	Bye!
Hello!	I am fine.	Good-bye!
	We are fine, thank you.	
Good morning!		So long!
Good afternoon!	How are you today?	Have a nice day!
	I am okay.	
Nice to meet you!	We are well, thanks.	See you later!

> **Pronouns**
>
> Use **I** to talk about yourself.
>   **I** am happy.
>
> Use **you** when you talk to someone else.
>   **You** are nice.
>
> Use **we** to talk about yourself and someone else.
>   **We** are friends.

B. Write what the people say. Use the chart.

1. Good morning!   Hello! _____

Greetings

2. How are you? _____

Question and Answer

3. _____   And how are you?

Question and Answer

4. _____   Good-bye! _____

Good-byes

      © NGSP & HB

Name _____

Who Is It?

▶ Grammar: Pronouns

When you talk about other people or things, use the correct pronoun.

 For a girl or a woman, use **she**.

She is a student.

 For a thing, use **it**.

It is a present.

 For a boy or a man, use **he**.

He is a student, too.

 Use **they** to talk about more than one person or thing.

They are friends.

Complete each sentence. Add the correct pronoun.

1. Josef and Mikka sit together.

   ___They___ are friends.

2. Mikka is 13 years old today.

   _____ is a teenager now.

3. Josef has a present for Mikka.

   _____ is a good friend.

4. Mikka likes surprises.

   _____ takes the present.

5. The present makes Mikka smile.

   _____ is a CD by her favorite band.

6. The friends laugh.

   _____ are happy.

They Are in a Race

► **Grammar: Present Tense Verbs: _Am, Is,_ and _Are_**

Use the verbs _am_, _is_, and _are_ correctly.

Pronoun	Verb	Example
I	am	I **am** in P.E. class.
he she it	is	He **is** slow. She **is** in front of me. It **is** a nice day.
we you they	are	We **are** happy. You **are** fast! They **are** outside.

Complete each sentence. Add the correct verb.

1.

I __am__ Lisa.

2.

She _____ in this race, too.

3.

He _____ behind us.

4.

I _____ not as fast as Jan.

5.

We say, "You _____ the winner, Jan!"

6.

Now we _____ ready to rest.

© NGSP & HB

Name _____

How Can You Communicate?

▶ **Vocabulary: Communication**

▶ **Language: Use the Telephone**

A. Name each picture. Use words from the box.

letter	fax	phone	e-mail

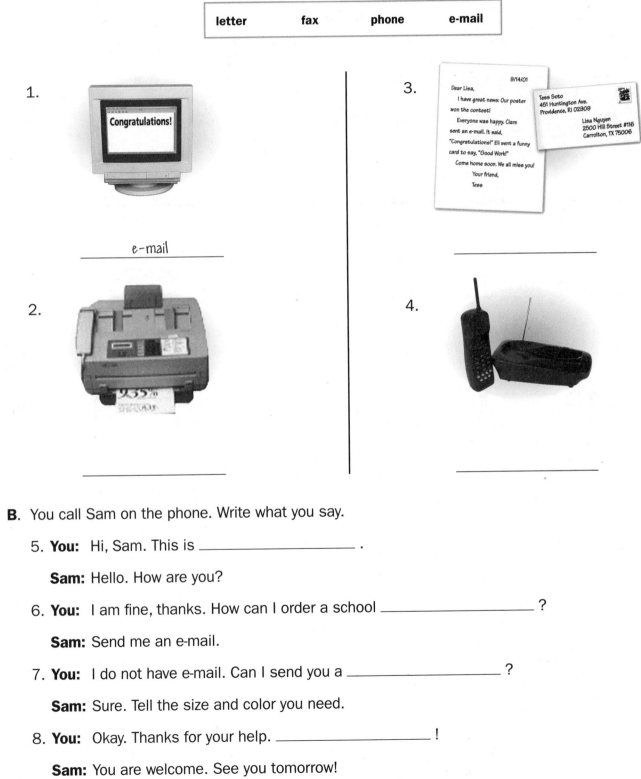

1. _____e-mail_____

3. _____

2. _____

4. _____

B. You call Sam on the phone. Write what you say.

5. **You:** Hi, Sam. This is _____ .

   Sam: Hello. How are you?

6. **You:** I am fine, thanks. How can I order a school _____ ?

   Sam: Send me an e-mail.

7. **You:** I do not have e-mail. Can I send you a _____ ?

   Sam: Sure. Tell the size and color you need.

8. **You:** Okay. Thanks for your help. _____ !

   Sam: You are welcome. See you tomorrow!

Identify Sequence

▶ **Sum It Up**

A. Read about good news. Then make a sequence chain. Tell who gets the good news and how they get it. Tell about events in order.

> **Good News from Manuel**
>
> Marta gets a letter from Cousin Manuel. It is good news! Cousin Manuel is coming to visit!
>
> Marta sends an e-mail to her brother Rico to tell him the good news. Rico sends a fax to Grandfather to tell him the good news. Grandfather calls Uncle Ciro on the phone to tell him the good news. The good news travels fast!

Marta – letter

↓

↓

↓

B. Read each question. Write the answers.

1. What is the good news? _____

2. Who gets the news first? _____

3. Does Grandfather or Uncle Ciro get the news from Rico? _____

4. Who gets the news last? _____

High Frequency Words, Part 1

A. Read each word. Then write it.

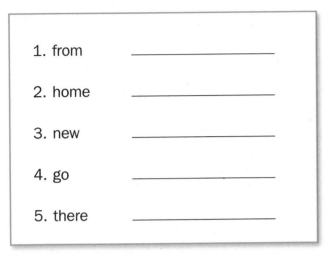

1. from   _____

2. home   _____

3. new   _____

4. go   _____

5. there   _____

B. Read each sentence. Find the new words in the box. Write the words on the lines.

6. These two words have an **m**.

_____ from _____   _____

7. This word has 3 letters.

_____

8. This word is the opposite of **stop**.

_____

9. This word rhymes with **where**.

_____

10. This word starts with **fr**.

_____

High Frequency Words, Part 2

A. Read each word. Then write it.

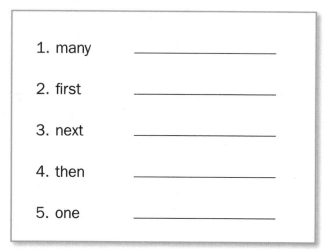

1. many   _____

2. first   _____

3. next   _____

4. then   _____

5. one   _____

B. Read each sentence. Find the new words in the box. Write the words on the lines.

6. This word has an **m**.

   _____ many _____

7. These 3 words tell "when."

   _____   _____   _____

8. This word has 3 letters.

   _____

9. These 3 words have 4 letters each.

   _____   _____   _____

10. This word has an **o**.

    _____

Language and Literacy

Words with Short *a* and Short *o*

A. Name each picture. Write the name.

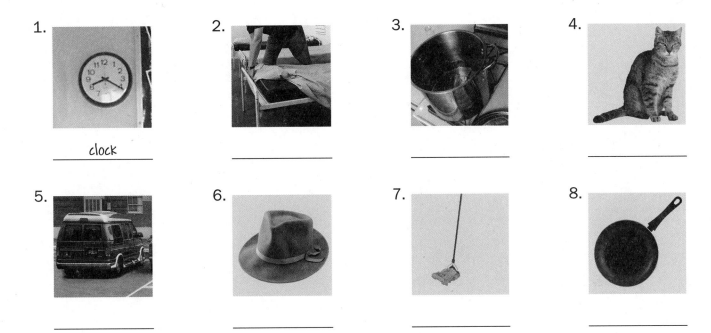

1. _____clock_____

2. _____

3. _____

4. _____

5. _____

6. _____

7. _____

8. _____

B. Now read the story. Circle the words with short *a* or short *o*. Write them in the chart. Write each word one time.

(Cat) Fun

Sam has a cat.

The cat has lots of fun.

It hops on the hat.

It naps in a pot.

It got into a pan.

It sleeps on the van.

When the cat is hot,

It jumps on the cot.

The cat can be bad.

But Sam likes his cat!

🐱		🕐	
9. ____cat____		18. _____	
10. _____		19. _____	
11. _____		20. _____	
12. _____		21. _____	
13. _____		22. _____	
14. _____		23. _____	
15. _____		24. _____	
16. _____			
17. _____			

Language and Literacy

Words with Short *a* and Short *o*

A. Name each picture. Write the name.

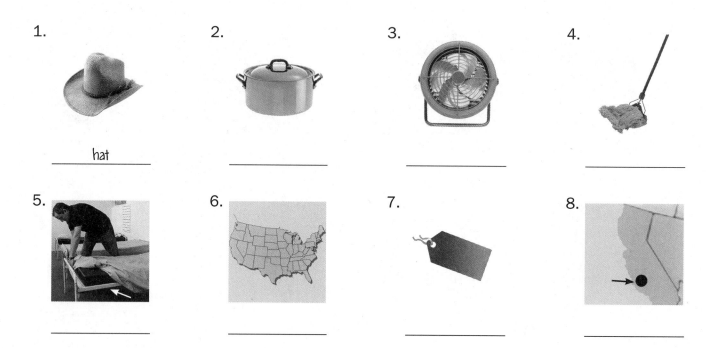

1. _____ hat _____

2. _____

3. _____

4. _____

5. _____

6. _____

7. _____

8. _____

B. Now read the story. Circle the words with short *a* or short *o*. Write them in the chart. Write each word one time.

I See a (Van)

I see a van.

It has a lot of things in it!

I see a map and a box in the van.

I see a mop and a fan in the van.

I see some pots and pans, too.

Is Tom in the van?

Tom is not in the van. There is no room!

9. _____ van _____	15. _____
10. _____	16. _____
11. _____	17. _____
12. _____	18. _____
13. _____	19. _____
14. _____	20. _____

Words with Short *a* and Short *o*

A. Read each word. Which picture goes with the word? Write its letter.

1. fan   *B*
2. box   ___
3. cap   ___
4. flag   ___
5. apple   ___

6. dot   ___
7. rock   ___
8. bat   ___
9. jog   ___
10. tag   ___

11. map   ___
12. spots   ___
13. ox   ___
14. cloth   ___
15. frog   ___

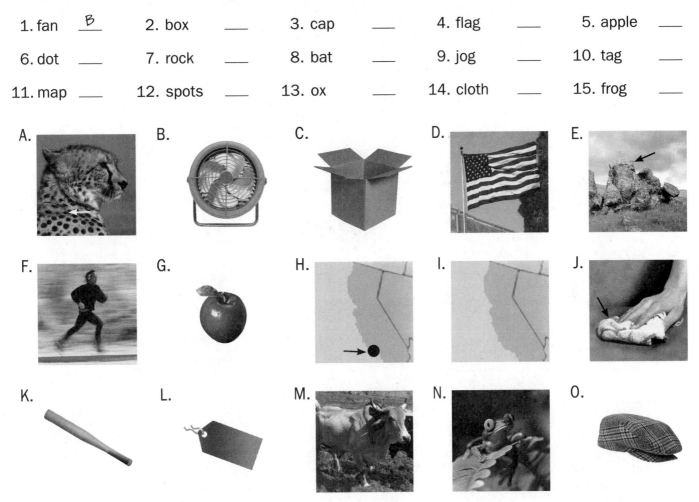

A.   B.   C.   D.   E.

F.   G.   H.   I.   J.

K.   L.   M.   N.   O.

B. Name each picture below. Which word or words above rhyme with the picture name? Write the words on the lines.

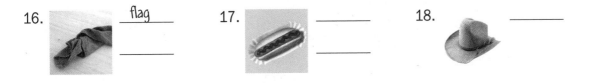

16. ___flag___ _____

17. _____ _____

18. _____

Language and Literacy

Words with Short *a* and Short *o*

A. Read each word. Which picture goes with the word? Write its letter.

1. cot *G*
2. cap ___
3. fan ___
4. top ___
5. jog ___

6. bag ___
7. fog ___
8. dot ___
9. van ___
10. rag ___

11. hop ___
12. bat ___
13. nap ___
14. hat ___
15. sad ___

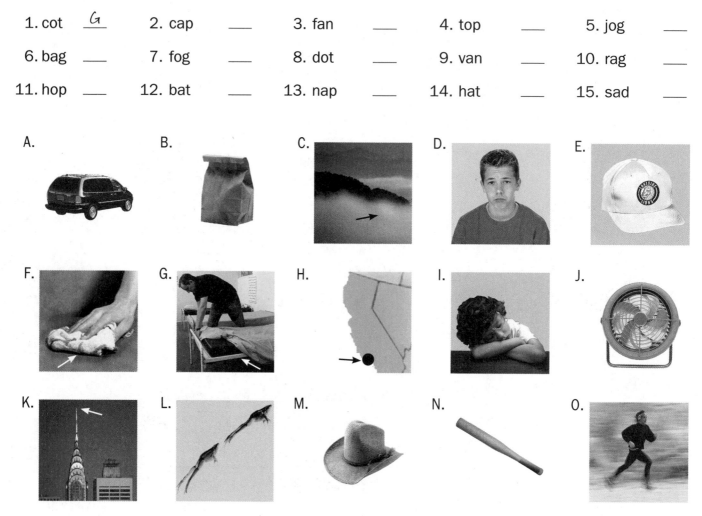

A. B. C. D. E.

F. G. H. I. J.

K. L. M. N. O.

B. Read each word. Find the word or words above that have the same vowel sound and spelling. Write the words on the lines.

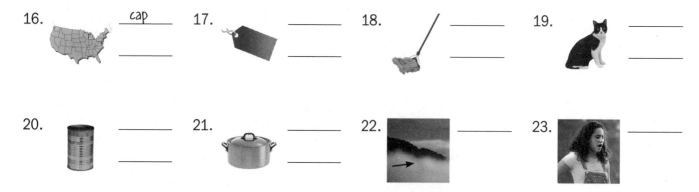

16. _*cap*_ ___
17. ___ ___
18. ___ ___
19. ___ ___

20. ___ ___
21. ___ ___
22. ___ ___
23. ___ ___

Language and Literacy

Build Reading Fluency

▶ Expression

A. Some sentences tell something. Other sentences show strong feeling.

This sentence tells something.
It ends with a period.

    Lupe is new at Lakeside School .

This sentence shows a strong feeling.
It ends with an exclamation mark.

    Lupe is glad to have 2 new friends !

B. Listen to the different kinds of sentences.

> **New at School**
>
> Lupe is new at Lakeside School.
> First she has science lab with Pat and Ron.
> Pat helps Lupe.
> They have many things to do.
> Next they have P.E. class.
> They go from one class to the next.
> Pat and Lupe go fast. Ron does not go fast.
> He has a cold and has to stop!
> Then Pat, Lupe, and Ron go to lunch.
> They have a lot of hot soup there.
> At last it is time to go home.
> Lupe is glad to have 2 new friends!

C. Now read the sentences above. Work with a partner. Say each kind of sentence with the right expression. See how your reading improves!

Language and Literacy

Everything Is New!

▶ Statements and Exclamations

A. Some sentences tell something. Other sentences show a strong feeling.

This sentence tells something. It ends with a period.

Vu has a new jacket .

All sentences start with a capital letter.

She goes to a new school today.

This sentence shows a strong feeling. It ends with an exclamation mark.

She loves it !

B. Complete each sentence. Start each sentence with a capital letter. Add a period or an exclamation mark at the end.

1. ___Vu___ opens her new locker.
   (Vu)

2. It is very small _____

3. She puts her jacket in it _____

4. Vu meets her new teacher _____

5. _____ teaches English.
   (he)

6. He is very tall _____

7. Vu walks home _____

8. _____ sees snow for the first time.
   (she)

9. She loves the snow _____

10. This is a great day _____

Learn Key Vocabulary

Many People to Meet: Key Vocabulary

A. Study each word. Circle a number to rate how well you know it. Then complete the chart.

Rating Scale	**1** I have never seen this word before.	**2** I am not sure of the word's meaning.	**3** I know this word and can teach the word's meaning to someone else.

▲ There are many **people** to **meet** in your neighborhood.

Key Words	Check Understanding	Deepen Understanding
❶ first (furst) *adverb* **Rating:** 1 2 3	If you are **first**, you are at the end of the line. Yes No	What is the first thing you say when you see a friend? _____ _____ _____ _____
❷ home (hōm) *noun* **Rating:** 1 2 3	A **home** can be a house or apartment. Yes No	Describe your home. _____ _____ _____ _____
❸ meet (mēt) *verb* **Rating:** 1 2 3	When you **meet** a friend for lunch, you sit together and talk while you eat. Yes No	Where do you meet friends? _____ _____ _____

Name _____

You **meet people** at school every day! ▶

Key Words	Check Understanding	Deepen Understanding
❹ next (nekst) *adverb* **Rating:** 1 2 3	I mail a letter. I put a stamp on it **next**. Yes No	Suppose you are next. How many people are in front of you? _____ _____ _____ _____
❺ people (pē-pul) *noun* **Rating:** 1 2 3	Boys and girls are **people**. Yes No	Name three people in your class. _____ _____ _____ _____

B. Use at least two of the Key Vocabulary words. Tell about a day when you met someone for the first time.

_____

_____

_____

Plan and Write

1. Who will you write to? What do you want to say?
   Make a list of names and possible topics.

   <u>Names</u>   <u>Topics</u>

   _____   _____

   _____   _____

   _____   _____

2. Choose a focus. Circle one name and topic.

Turn your ideas into sentences. Write your e-mail.

3. Fill in your friend's name after To:

4. Fill in your name after From:

5. Fill in the date after Sent:

6. Fill in the topic after Subject:

7. Write a greeting.

8. Write your message. Share your news.

9. Write a closing like *Love*, *See you soon*, or *Your friend*. Use a comma after the closing.

10. Write your name.

To: _____

From: _____

Sent: _____

Subject: _____

Hi _____,

How are you? I am _____. I have news for you.

I _____

_____

_____

_____

_____

Check Your Work

▶ Capitalization and End Marks

Read the e-mail. Fix capital letters and end punctuation as needed.
Mark your changes. Then write the sentences correctly.

To: robert@teenschool.com

From: Luis

Sent: October 5, 2008

Subject: My soccer team

Hi Robert,

How are you? I am great I joined a soccer team at school. We are called the Wildcats. We

practice three times a week We had our first game last Wednesday. our team won 2 to 1.

I scored one point! I wish you were on my team write back soon.

Your friend,

Luis

_____

_____

_____

_____

_____

_____

_____

_____

_____

_____

Mind Map

Use the mind map to show what you know about food. As you read the
selections in this unit, add new ideas you learn about different types of food.

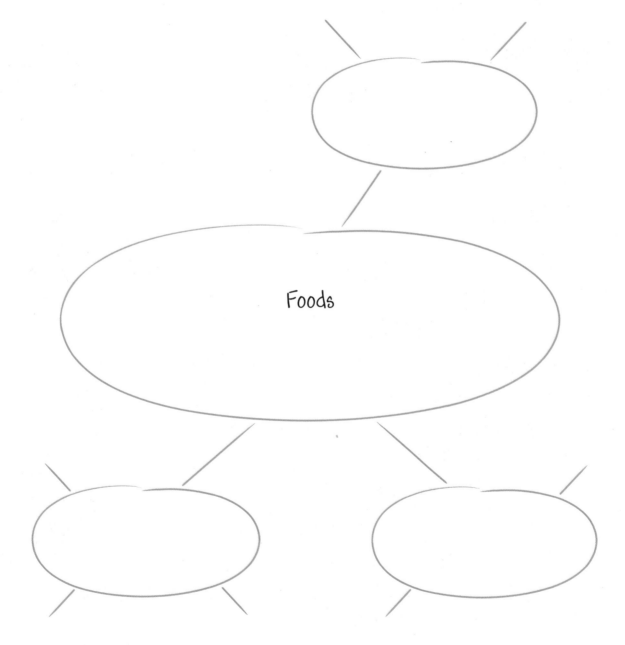

Name _____

Lunch Looks Good!

▶ **Vocabulary: Colors, Shapes, and Sizes**

▶ **Language: Describe**

A. Look at each picture. Tell the size or shape. Use a word from the box.

small	round	square	long	triangular	rectangular

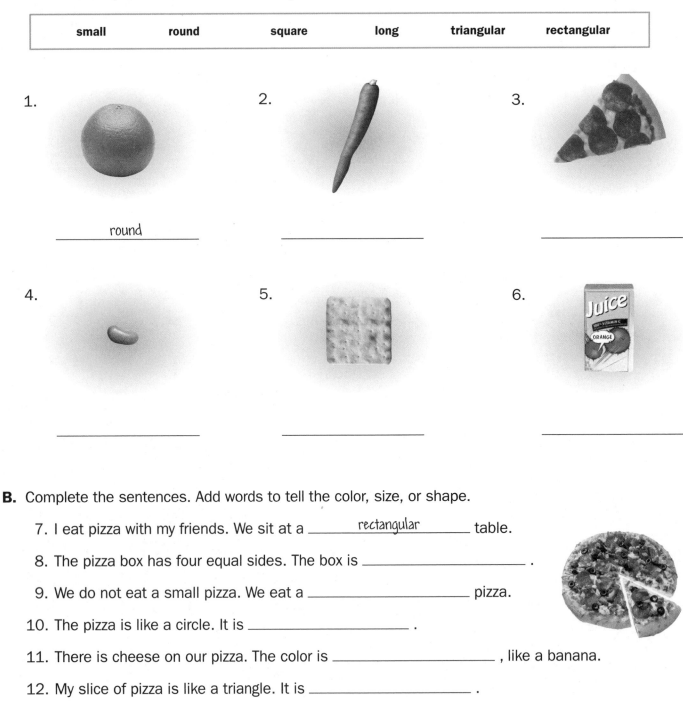

1. _____round_____

2. _____

3. _____

4. _____

5. _____

6. _____

B. Complete the sentences. Add words to tell the color, size, or shape.

7. I eat pizza with my friends. We sit at a _____rectangular_____ table.

8. The pizza box has four equal sides. The box is _____ .

9. We do not eat a small pizza. We eat a _____ pizza.

10. The pizza is like a circle. It is _____ .

11. There is cheese on our pizza. The color is _____ , like a banana.

12. My slice of pizza is like a triangle. It is _____ .

What's for Lunch?

▶ **Vocabulary: Foods**

▶ **Language: Describe**

A. Name each food. Use words from the box.

| butter | chicken | milk | plum | pear | peas | roll | water |

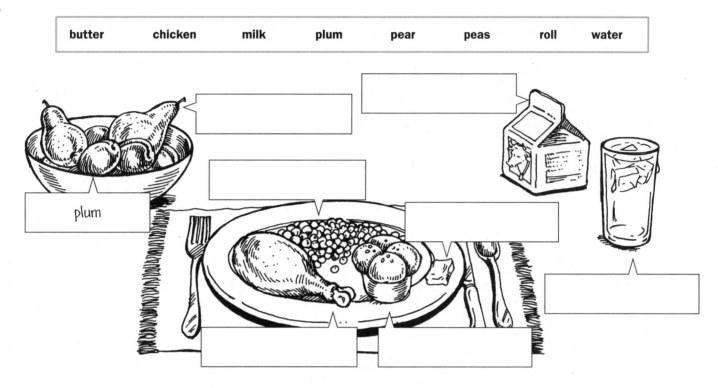

plum

B. Complete each sentence. Tell about the food. Then name it.

1. This is a kind of bread. You can put _____butter_____ on it. It is a _____roll_____ .

2. This is a cold drink. It is in a tall _____ . It is _____ .

3. These are green. They are _____ in size. They are _____ .

4. This is a fruit. It has a _____ shape. It is a _____ .

Language Development

Let's Eat Salad

▶ Grammar: Action Verbs

An action verb tells what someone does.

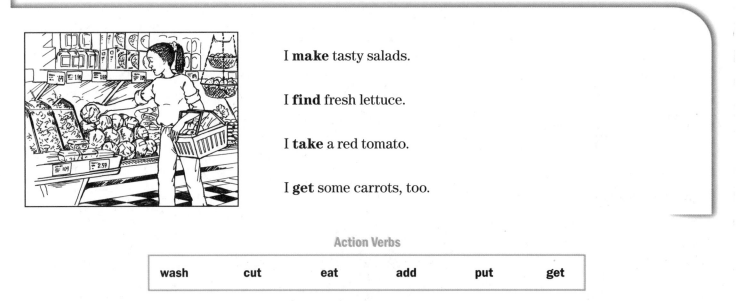

I **make** tasty salads.

I **find** fresh lettuce.

I **take** a red tomato.

I **get** some carrots, too.

Action Verbs

wash	cut	eat	add	put	get

Complete each sentence. Tell how to make a salad. Use verbs from the box.

1.

I ____wash____ the lettuce.

2.

I _____ some carrots.

3.

I _____ the tomato.

4.

I _____ the salad in a bowl.

5.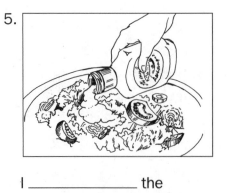

I _____ the dressing.

6.

I _____ the salad!

Name _____

Identify Steps in a Process

▶ Sum It Up

A. Think about how to make a hamburger. Put the steps in order.

_____ Put the burger on a bun.

_____ Shape the meat into a round burger.

_____ Cook the burger.

__l__ Put meat, onions, egg, salt, and pepper in a bowl.

_____ Mix the ingredients together.

B. Use the steps to make a sequence chain. Tell about how to make a hamburger.

Put meat, onions, egg, salt, and pepper in a bowl.

↓

↓

↓

↓

High Frequency Words, Part 1

A. Read each word. Then write it.

1. something _____

2. make _____

3. long _____

4. large _____

5. move _____

B. Read the clue. Write the word in the chart. Then write the word again in the sentence.

What to Look For	Word	Sentence
6. has the word **some** in it	s o m e t h i n g	I want _something_ hot.
7. rhymes with **take**	__ __ __ __	You _____ great food.
8. rhymes with **song**	__ __ __ __	I like _____ noodles.
9. means "big"	__ __ __ __ __	You have a _____ bag.
10. ends with **ve**	__ __ __ __	Please _____ over.

Name _____

High Frequency Words, Part 2

A. Read each word. Then write it.

1. different   _____

2. small   _____

3. open   _____

4. same   _____

5. eat   _____

B. Read the clue. Write the word in the chart. Then write the word again in the sentence.

What to Look For	Word	Sentence
6. has **ff**	d i f f e r e n t	Your bag is ____different____ .
7. starts with **sm**	__ __ __ __ __	My lunch is in a _____ bag.
8. starts with **o**	__ __ __ __	I _____ my lunch bag.
9. ends with **me**	__ __ __ __	Our food is not the _____ .
10. has three letters	__ __ __	It is time to _____ .

Language and Literacy

Words with Short *i* and Short *u*

A. Name each picture. Write the name.

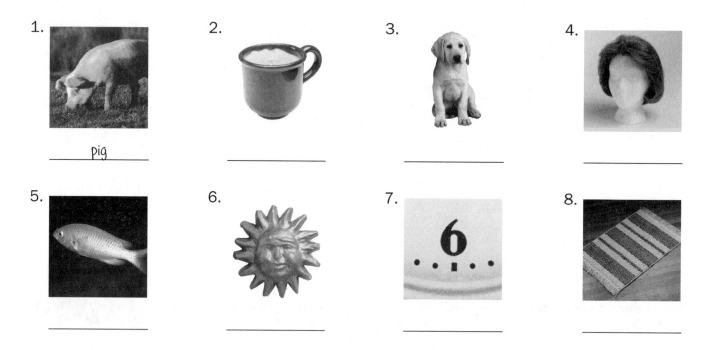

1. _____ pig _____

2. _____

3. _____

4. _____

5. _____

6. _____

7. _____

8. _____

B. Now read the story. Circle the words with short *i* or short *u*. Write them in the chart. Write each word one time.

My New (Pup)

Yesterday I got a new pup.
She sips milk from a little cup.
We sit in the sun.
Then we go for a run.
I know one day my pup will get big.
I hope she never looks like a pig!
For now I just love my silly mutt.

9. _____	15. ___ pup ___
10. _____	16. _____
11. _____	17. _____
12. _____	18. _____
13. _____	19. _____
14. _____	20. _____
	21. _____
	22. _____
	23. _____

Name _____

Words with Short *i* and Short *u*

A. Name each picture. Write the name.

1. _____pin_____

2. _____

3. _____

4. _____

5. _____

6. _____

7. _____

8. _____

B. Now read the story. Circle the words with short *i* or short *u*. Write them in the chart. Write each word one time.

(Just) Great!

Sam needs something to eat.
He rips open a bag of chips.
The chips are good, but not great.
Sam cuts a bit of ham and
slaps it on a bun.
The ham is good, but not great.
Mom comes in.
She gets a cup of ice cream.
She adds lots of nuts.
Sam grins. Yes! That is great!

9. _____Just_____	15. _____
10. _____	16. _____
11. _____	17. _____
12. _____	18. _____
13. _____	19. _____
14. _____	20. _____
	21. _____

Words with Short *i* and Short *u*

A. Read each word. Which picture goes with the word? Write its letter.

1. cup _G_
2. fin ___
3. pump ___
4. hit ___
5. sit ___

6. rug ___
7. disk ___
8. nut ___
9. pig ___
10. dig ___

11. sun ___
12. pin ___
13. cut ___
14. lid ___
15. bun ___

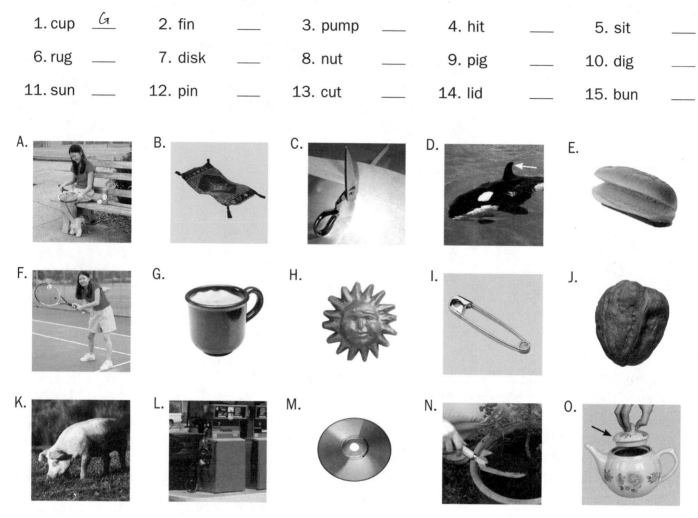

A. B. C. D. E.

F. G. H. I. J.

K. L. M. N. O.

B. Name each picture below. Which word or words above rhyme with the picture name? Write the words on the lines.

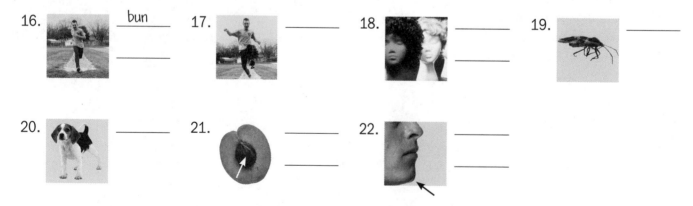

16. _bun_ ___
17. ___
18. ___
19. ___

20. ___
21. ___
22. ___

Words with Short *i* and Short *u*

A. Write the missing letters. Then read the words in each list. How are the words different?

1.

p __ __ __

__ __ __

__ __ __

2.

__ __ __

__ __ __

__ __ __

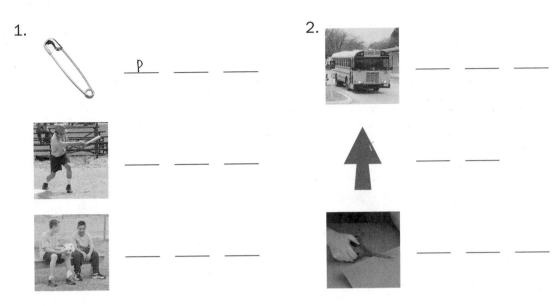

B. Read each question. What word goes in the answer? Spell the word. Then circle the correct picture.

3. Where is the cup? The __c__ ____ ____ is here.

4. Who made a hit? John made a ____ ____ ____ .

5. Where is the first-aid kit? The first-aid ____ ____ ____ is here.

6. Where is the pup? The ____ ____ ____ is here.

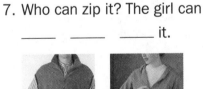

7. Who can zip it? The girl can ____ ____ ____ it.

8. Where is the fish? Here is the ____ ____ ____ .

Build Reading Fluency

▶ **Phrasing**

A. When you read, pause between groups of words that go together.

Kim likes hot dogs / for lunch.
She cooks / a batch of hot dogs / in a big pot.

B. Listen to the story. Which groups of words does the reader say together? Where does he pause? When you hear a pause, write a /.

Example: Kim likes hot dogs / for lunch.

Something Good for Lunch

Kim likes hot dogs for lunch.
She cooks a batch of hot dogs in a big pot.
Next Kim chops some small onions.
She opens a large bag of buns.
She fills the buns with hot dogs, mustard, and onions.
She opens a bag of chips, too.
She pours a cup of punch.
This is too much food to eat!
Kim calls Mitch.
Then they sit and eat a great lunch!

B. Now read the story to a partner. Read groups of words together. Pause when you see a /.

I Am Not a Cook!

▶ Negative Sentences

A. A negative sentence has a negative word, like *not*.

The fish is **not** big.
The carrots are **not** long.
Meg is **not** happy.

B. Look at each picture. Complete the sentence.
Add a verb and the word *not*.

1.

I ____am____ ____not____ a
good cook.

2.

The forks _____ _____
clean.

3.

The plates _____
_____ on the table.

4.

The pasta _____ _____
in the water.

5.

The rolls _____ _____
hot.

6.

Dinner _____ _____
ready!

Learn Key Vocabulary

U.S. Tour of Food: Key Vocabulary

A. Study each word. Circle a number to rate how well you know it. Then complete the chart.

▲ Fruit comes in different **colors, shapes,** and **sizes.**

Rating Scale	**1** I have never seen this word before.	**2** I am not sure of the word's meaning.	**3** I know this word and can teach the word's meaning to someone else.

Key Words	Check Understanding	Deepen Understanding
❶ color (kuh-ler) *noun* **Rating:** 1 2 3	Purple is a dark **color**. Yes No	What color do you like best? _____ _____ _____ _____
❷ foods (fūdz) *noun* **Rating:** 1 2 3	Paper and pens are **foods**. Yes No	Name two foods that you like a lot. _____ _____ _____ _____
❸ shapes (shāps) *noun* **Rating:** 1 2 3	Apples and oranges have round **shapes**. Yes No	Name some shapes. _____ _____ _____ _____

Key Vocabulary, continued

There are many kinds of **foods** at a farmers' market. ▶

Key Words	Check Understanding	Deepen Understanding
4 sizes (sīzez) *noun* **Rating:** 1 2 3	Grapes and shrimp have small **sizes**. Yes No	What are some sizes of nuts? _____ _____ _____ _____
5 visit (vi-zit) *verb* **Rating:** 1 2 3	Friends may **visit** each other. Yes No	What people do you visit? _____ _____ _____ _____

B. Use at least two of the Key Vocabulary words. Describe foods you ate at your last meal.

_____

_____

_____

Writing Project

Plan and Write

1. What art can you make with food? Make a list. Draw pictures of what the food will look like.

Food: _____	Food: _____	Food: _____

2. Choose one idea for your How-To Card. Put a check mark next to the one you choose.

3. Think about the food you need. Plan each step. Write each step.

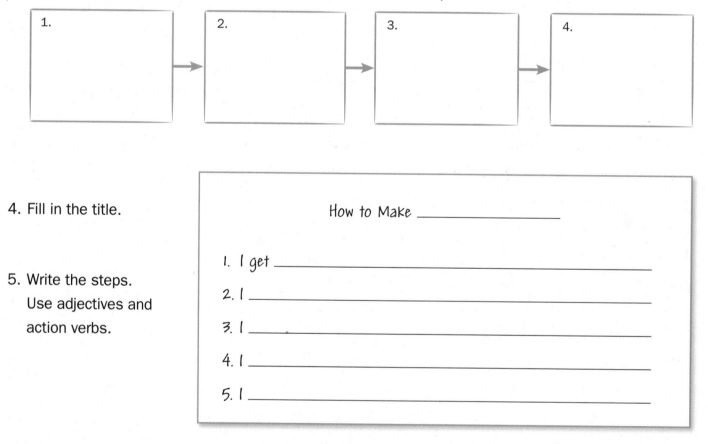

1.	→	2.	→	3.	→	4.

4. Fill in the title.

5. Write the steps.
   Use adjectives and
   action verbs.

How to Make _____

1. I get _____

2. I _____

3. I _____

4. I _____

5. I _____

Check Your Work

► Capitalization and Adding Words

Read the How-To Card. Fix capital letters. Add an action verb if one is missing from a step. Add adjectives to tell color, shape, or how many. Mark your changes.

Mark Your Changes

∧ Add.

≡ Capitalize.

How to Make a Rabbit Face

1. i put a pear half on a plate.

2. then I add peach slices for ears.

3. I coconut for the rabbit's fur.

4. I put raisins for eyes.

5. last, I add a cherry for the nose.

Draw a picture of what the finished rabbit face might look like.

Name _____

Mind Map

Use the mind map to show workers at school, their jobs, and the tools they use to do their jobs. As you read the selections in this unit, add new ideas you learn about the work that people do.

Worker	Job	Tools

Tell About the Jobs They Do

▶ **Language: Give Information**
▶ **Vocabulary: Actions and Careers**

A. Study the charts.

Careers	Actions
artist	draw
cab driver	drive
carpenter	build

Careers	Actions
gardener	plant
police officer	protect
teacher	teach

B. Complete each sentence. Use the chart.

1.

He is an ___artist___ .

He can ___draw___ and paint.

2.

She is a _____ .

She can _____ things.

3.

Here is a _____ .

She can _____ flowers.

4.

She can _____ us.

She is a _____ .

5.

He is a _____ .

He can _____ us how to write.

6.

This is a _____ .

He can _____ people places.

Everyone Helps

▶ **Grammar: Present Tense Verbs**

To tell what another person or thing does, use a verb that ends in **-s**.

The Ali family **owns** a store.

It **keeps** them busy.

Mr. Ali **works** hard.

Mrs. Ali **helps**.

Read each sentence. Add the correct form of the action verb.

1.

Mr. Ali _____cleans_____ .
(clean)

He _____ the sidewalk.
(sweep)

2.

He _____ a box for Mr. Ali.
(move)

It _____ fresh apples.
(hold)

3.

Mrs. Ali _____ the money.
(take)

She _____ the man.
(thank)

4.

Kira _____ a flower.
(cut)

She _____ it in water.
(put)

What Tools Do They Use?

▶ **Vocabulary: Tools and Careers**

▶ **Language: Ask and Answer Questions**

A. Name the tool each worker has. Use words from the box.

| brush | pencil | notebook | wrench | paper | computer | scissors |

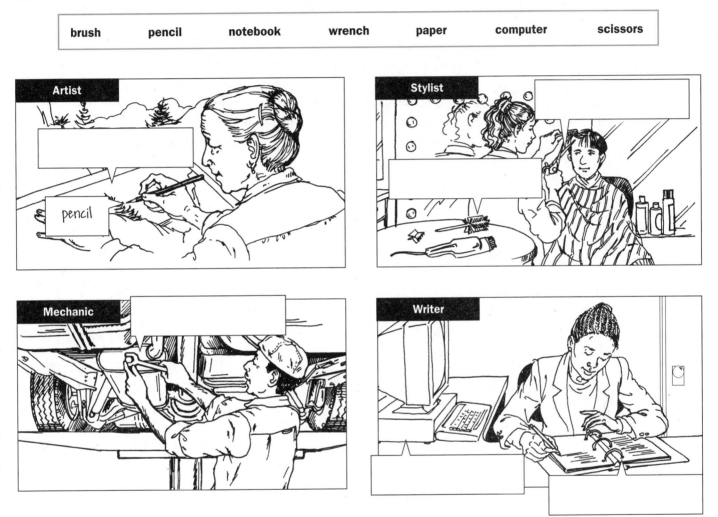

B. Look at the pictures above. Read each question. Write the answer.

1. Can the artist draw?

   Yes, she can.
   _____

2. Is the writer in an office?

   _____

3. Are the stylist and the boy in a garage?

   _____

4. Is the notebook open?

   _____

5. Can the mechanic use a wrench?

   _____

6. Is the wrench on the floor?

   _____

Language Development

Name _____

Identify Details

▶ **Sum It Up**

A. Read about Hana's morning. Then make a concept web to show the people who help her.

> ### Hana's Helpers
>
> Hana is in a hurry to get to class. She leaves her library book on the bus. The bus driver finds the book. He gives it to the custodian. The custodian takes the book to the school office. An office worker takes the book to Hana's teacher.
>
> Hana's teacher gives the book back to Hana. Hana is happy to get the book! That afternoon, Hana takes the book to the library. The librarian helps Hana renew the book so she can finish reading it.

bus driver

Who Helps Hana?

B. Finish the paragraph. Use details from your concept web.

Hana wants to thank everyone who helped her. She starts by thanking the

_____librarian_____ who helps her renew the book. Then Hana goes to the classroom

and thanks her _____ . As Hana gets on the bus to go home, she thanks

the _____ . The next morning, Hana thanks the _____

and the _____ at school.

Language and Literacy

High Frequency Words, Part 1

A. Read each word. Then write it.

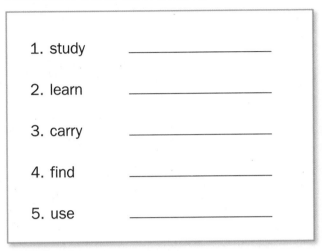

1. study   _____

2. learn   _____

3. carry   _____

4. find   _____

5. use   _____

B. Read each sentence. Find the new words in the box.
Write the words on the lines.

6. This word starts with **st**.

_____ study _____

7. This word starts with **l**.

_____

8. These 3 words have 5 letters each.

_____ _____ _____

9. This word has an **i**.

_____

10. This word ends with **e**.

_____

Name _____

High Frequency Words, Part 2

A. Read each word. Then write it.

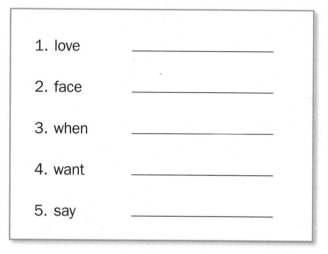

1. love   _____

2. face   _____

3. when   _____

4. want   _____

5. say   _____

B. Read each sentence. Find the new words in the box. Write the words on the lines.

6. This word starts with **l**.

   _____ love _____

7. These 2 words end with **e**.

   _____   _____

8. This word rhymes with **then**.

   _____

9. This word ends with **nt**.

   _____

10. This word rhymes with **day**.

   _____

Name _____

Words with Short e

A. Read each word. Which picture goes with the word? Write its letter.

1. web _G_
2. fence ___
3. bell ___

4. desk ___
5. ten ___
6. hen ___

7. egg ___
8. vest ___
9. leg ___

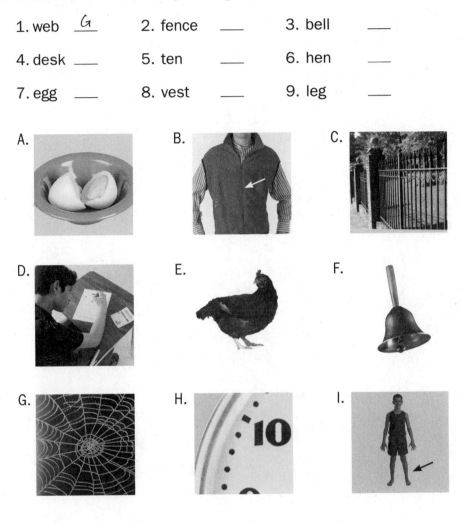

A.   B.   C.

D.   E.   F.

G.   H.   I.

B. Read each sentence. Write the correct word on the line.

10. This word rhymes with **best**.

_____

11. This word rhymes with **tell**.

_____

Words with Short e

A. Read each word. Which picture goes with the word? Write its letter.

1. hen _F_   2. check ___   3. net ___   4. pet ___

5. bed ___   6. chest ___   7. pen ___   8. vet ___

9. egg ___   10. bench ___   11. stretch ___   12. send ___

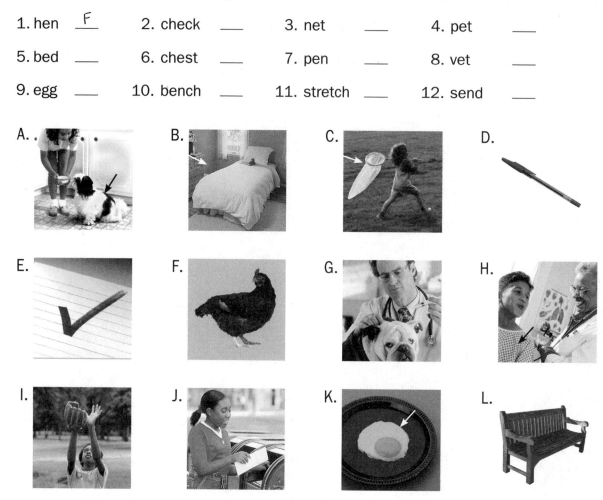

A.   B.   C.   D.

E.   F.   G.   H.

I.   J.   K.   L.

B. Name each picture below. Which words above rhyme with the picture name? Write the words on the lines.

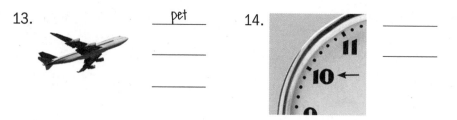

13. ___pet___
    _____
    _____

14. _____
    _____

Final *ll, ss, zz, ck*

A. Read each word. Which picture goes with the word? Write its letter.

1. chick _A_   2. pill ___   3. bell ___   4. fizz ___

5. check ___   6. jazz ___   7. kiss ___   8. spill ___

9. rock ___   10. sick ___   11. dress ___   12. hill ___

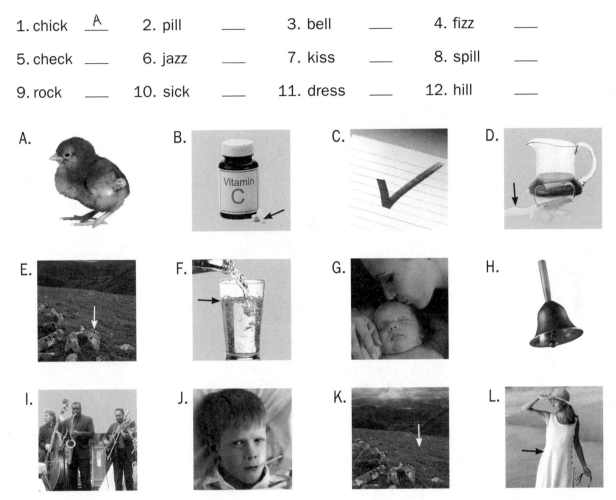

A.   B.   C.   D.

E.   F.   G.   H.

I.   J.   K.   L.

B. Name each picture below. What is the last sound? Find the words above that have the same sound at the end. Write the words on the lines.

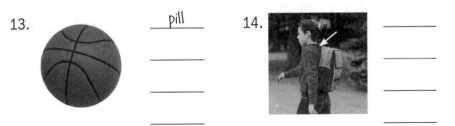

13.   _pill_
       _____
       _____
       _____

14.   _____
       _____
       _____

Words with *sh*

A. Read each word. Which picture goes with the word? Write its letter.

1. shirt _B_   2. fish ___   3. trash ___

4. ship ___   5. shell ___   6. shoulder ___

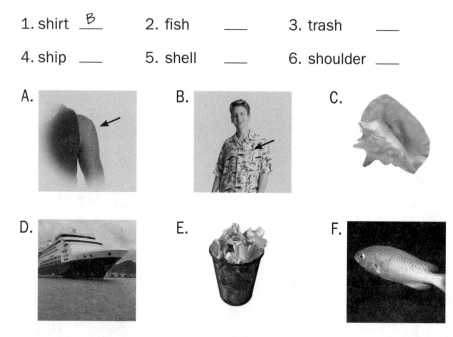

A.   B.   C.

D.   E.   F.

B. Now read the story. Circle the words with the *sh* sound. Write the words in the chart. Write each word one time.

(Shiny) New Shoes

I have a pair of shiny new shoes. They are

a pale shade of blue. I think the shoelaces

are too short. After school, I will take them

back to the shop. I will show the laces to the

salesman. I will not be shy. Tonight I will put

my new shoes on a shelf. I will shut the door

and go to sleep.

7. shiny	12.
8.	13.
9.	14.
10.	15.
11.	16.

Build Reading Fluency

► **Intonation**

A. Some sentences ask something. Other sentences show strong feeling.

This sentence asks a question.
It ends with a question mark.

> Do you want to send something **?**

This sentence shows a strong feeling.
It ends with an exclamation mark.

> Then he hops on his bike and … zip **!**

B. Listen to the reader's voice. Listen for sentences that ask a question or show a strong feeling.

Let Ben Take It

Ben is a bike messenger.
Do you want to send something?
Ben can get it there fast.
Just say where it must go.
He gets his map.
He can study it to learn the best route.
He uses it to find a shop.
Then he hops on his bike and … zip!
He is off like a jet.
Ben can carry a lot of different things:
food, pictures, letters, flowers.
They fit in the big bag on his back.
Ben loves his job.
He has a smile on his face.
When you want to send something,
let Ben take it!

C. Now read the sentences to a partner. See how your reading improves!

Who? What? Where? When?

▶ **Questions with *Who, What, Where,* and *When***

A. You can use the words *Who, What, Where,* or *When* to start a question.

Use *Who* to ask about a person.

    Who is this?

Use *What* to ask about a thing.

    What is his job?

Use *Where* to ask about a place.

    Where can he go?

Use *When* to ask about a time.

    When is he at work?

B. Complete each question. Use *Who, What, Where,* or *When*.

1. __Who__ drives the cab?
   Mr. Siwela drives the cab.

2. _____ is on his head?
   A cap is on his head.

3. _____ is the cab?
   The cab is at the flower shop.

4. _____ is the shop?
   The shop is on Main Street.

5. _____ wants a ride in the cab?
   Ms. Vega wants a ride.

6. _____ is in her hand?
   A plant is in her hand.

7. _____ is she ready to go?
   She is ready to go now.

8. _____ is her home?
   Her home is on Elm Street.

Learn Key Vocabulary

Name _____

Geologists–Rock Scientists: Key Vocabulary

A. Study each word. Circle a number to rate how well you know it. Then complete the chart.

Rating Scale	**1** I have never seen this word before.	**2** I am not sure of the word's meaning.	**3** I know this word and can teach the word's meaning to someone else.

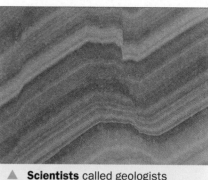

▲ **Scientists** called geologists can tell how old this **rock** is by **studying** its layers.

Key Words	Check Understanding	Deepen Understanding
❶ **learn** (lurn) *verb* **Rating:** 1 2 3	To become a doctor, you must **learn** about the human body. **Yes** **No**	What do you like to learn about? _____ _____ _____ _____
❷ **rock** (rok) *noun* **Rating:** 1 2 3	Most kinds of **rock** are soft. **Yes** **No**	Describe a kind of rock in your area. _____ _____ _____ _____
❸ **scientist** (si-yun-tist) *noun* **Rating:** 1 2 3	A **scientist** studies nature. **Yes** **No**	Name a kind of scientist. _____ _____ _____ _____

Name _____

Scientists use tools to find clues in **rocks** about the past. ▶

Key Words	Check Understanding	Deepen Understanding
④ study (stuh-dē) *verb* **Rating:** 1 2 3	When you **study** science, you learn about plants and animals. Yes No	What will you study today? _____ _____ _____ _____
⑤ use (yūz) *verb* **Rating:** 1 2 3	Chefs **use** pots and pans. Yes No	What tools do farmers use? _____ _____ _____ _____

B. Use at least two of the Key Vocabulary words. Imagine you are a geologist. What would your day be like?

_____

_____

_____

Plan and Write

1. What worker will you interview? Name the worker's job. _____

2. What do you want to know? Make a list.

   _____   _____

   _____   _____

   _____   _____

3. Choose a focus. Check three items.

4. Turn your ideas into questions. Write the questions. End each question with a **question mark.** Leave room for answers.

Q: What is _____

A: My name is _____

_____

Q: Where do _____

A: I work _____

_____

Q: What is _____

A: _____

_____

Q: What do you like _____

A: I like _____

_____

Q: _____

A: _____

_____

---

5. Study the questions. Interview a worker. Write your answers and get a photo or draw a picture of the person.

Check Your Work

▶ **Capitalization and End Marks**

Read the interview. Fix capital letters and end marks where they are needed. Mark your changes. Then write the sentences correctly.

Animal Doctor

Q: what is your name and what is your job

_____

A: my name is Martin Lee and I am an animal doctor

_____

Q: where do you work

_____

A: i work in an animal hospital on Park Street

_____

Q: what made you want to do this job

_____

A: i have always loved animals i lived on a farm when I was growing up

_____

_____

Q: what do you like best about your job

_____

A: my favorite thing is seeing animals get better my work makes people happy, too that's because pets are very important to people

_____

_____

_____

Name _____

Mind Map

Use the mind map to show the different things that numbers can tell you. As you read the selections in this unit, add new ideas you learn about how numbers are used.

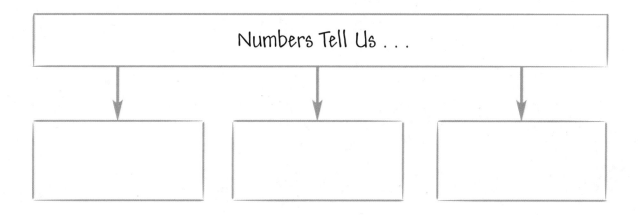

What Questions Do They Ask?

▶ **Language: Ask Questions**

▶ **Grammar: Questions with *Do* and *Does***

Complete each question. Then complete the answer.
Use *do* or *does*.

1. _Do_ I need two caps? / No, you _____ not.

2. _____ you have five bats? / Yes, we _____ .

3. _____ it cost ten dollars? / Yes, it _____ .

4. _____ Marco work here? / No, he _____ not.

Numbers Tell How Many

▶ **Vocabulary: Cardinal Numbers**
▶ **Language: Give Information**

A. Read the number words. Write the numbers.

1. four thousand, five hundred forty _____4,540_____

2. nine hundred ninety-seven _____

3. three hundred ten thousand _____

4. two million, one hundred thousand _____

5. fifty-four thousand, one hundred one _____

6. eight hundred thirty-eight _____

7. five thousand, six hundred fourteen _____

8. seven hundred nineteen _____

9. thirty million, two hundred thousand _____

10. ten thousand, four hundred one _____

B. Complete the facts about this student's school. Use number words.

11. My school ___has three fields_____ .
                          (3 fields)

12. My school _____ .
                          (12 classrooms)

13. My school _____
                          (24 computers)

                  _____ .

14. My school _____
                          (347 students)

                  _____ .

I Am Not Ready!

▶ Grammar: Negative Sentences

There are different ways to build negative sentences.

Add **not** after **am, is,** or **are**.

I am not late.

I am late!

He is ready.　　　He is not ready.

Add **do not** or **does not** before other verbs.

I have my bag.

I do not have my bag!

He gets on the bus.　　　He does not get on the bus.

A. Make each sentence a negative sentence. Use a verb and the word *not*.

1. I am ready for the game.

   I _____*am not*_____ ready for the game.

2. The bus is on time.

   The bus _____ on time.

3. We are on Bus 5.

   We _____ on Bus 5.

B. Make each sentence a negative sentence. Add *do not* or *does not*.

4. The bus driver leaves at 4:00.

   The bus driver _____ at 4:00.

5. She closes the doors.

   She _____ the doors.

6. The players go to the game.

   The players _____ to the game.

First, Second, Third . . .

▶ **Vocabulary: Ordinal Numbers**

▶ **Language: Express Needs**

A. Look at the picture. In what order are the people?
Write words from the box to show the order.

first	second	third	fourth	fifth	sixth	seventh	eighth	ninth	tenth

first

My bag does not have a tag.

I am hungry!

B. Use the picture above to complete each sentence. Tell what the person needs.

mother	sneakers	bag	food	tag

1. The first person needs ___sneakers___ .

2. The fourth person needs a _____ .

3. The sixth person needs a big _____ .

4. The seventh person needs his _____ .

5. The tenth person needs _____ .

Identify Problem and Solution

▶ Sum It Up

Read the story. Complete the problem-and-solution chart. Use your chart to retell the story to a partner.

> **Friends to the Rescue**
>
> Morris opened his lunch bag as he talked to his friends. Suddenly, his face changed. He pulled out two small toy trucks.
>
> "Oh, no," Morris groaned. "I picked up the wrong bag. This is what my mom bought for my little brother. I don't have anything to eat."
>
> "You can have half of my peanut butter and jelly sandwich," said Pam.
>
> "Here, take some of these. I can't eat all these grapes," said Jeff.
>
> "I'll share my carton of juice with you," offered Jack.
>
> "Thanks, everybody," Morris said. "What teamwork!"

Problem-and-Solution Chart

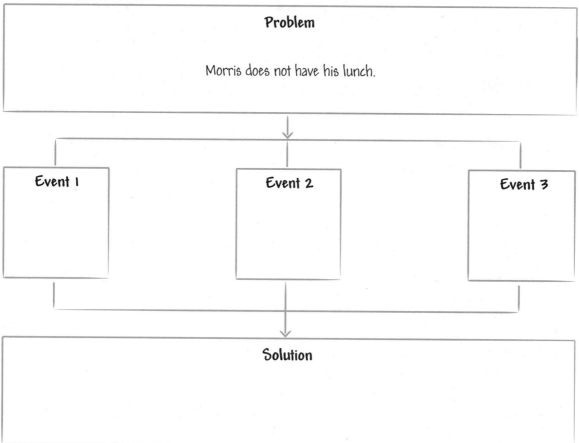

Problem

Morris does not have his lunch.

Event 1

Event 2

Event 3

Solution

Language and Literacy

High Frequency Words, Part 1

A. Read each word. Then write it.

1. leave _____

2. two _____

3. out _____

4. three _____

5. all _____

B. Work with a partner. Follow the steps.

- Read aloud each new word in the box.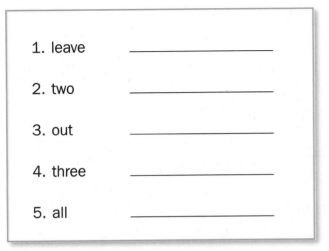

- Your partner writes the words.

- Have your partner read the words to you.

- Now you write the words on the lines below.

- Read the words to your partner.

6. _____

7. _____

8. _____

9. _____

10. _____

High Frequency Words, Part 2

A. Read each word. Then write it.

1. says _____

2. second _____

3. without _____

4. enough _____

5. more _____

B. Find the new words in the box. Write the words on the lines.

6. These 2 words begin with **s**.

_____ says _____   _____

C. Work with a partner. Follow the steps.

• Read aloud each new word in the box.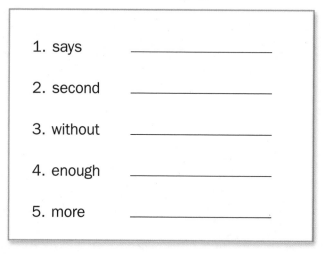

• Your partner writes the words.

• Have your partner read the words to you.

• Now you write the words on the lines below.

• Read the words to your partner.

7. _____

8. _____

9. _____

10. _____

11. _____

Name _____

Words with Digraphs

A. Name each picture. Write the name.

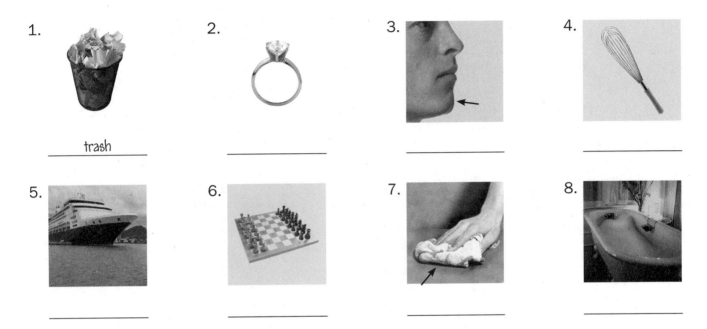

1. trash

2. _____

3. _____

4. _____

5. _____

6. _____

7. _____

8. _____

B. Now read the story. Circle the words that go in the chart. Write them in the chart. Write each word one time.

A Trip to (the) (Shop)

Dad and I go out to a shop. I think it sells great shells. We can bring some to Mom. I pick six shells and Dad pays cash. There is one more thing we want to do – find some fresh fish to eat. When we go home, Dad gives Mom the shells. Mom loves them and puts them on a shelf. What a great day!

Starts with *th*	Starts with *sh*
9. the	16. Shop
10. _____	17. _____
11. _____	18. _____
12. _____	
13. _____	

Ends with *ng*	Ends with *sh*
14. _____	19. _____
15. _____	20. _____
	21. _____

Name _____

Words with Blends and Digraphs

A. Name each picture. Write the name.

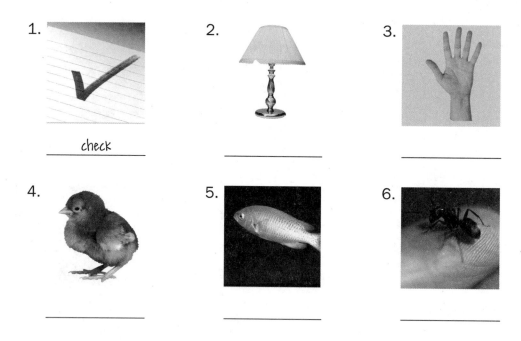

1. _____check_____

2. _____

3. _____

4. _____

5. _____

6. _____

B. Now read the story. Circle the words that go in the chart. Write them in the chart. Write each word one time.

Sal's Big (Trunk)

Sal has a big trunk. He fills it with things.

Open the trunk and look in. You will see five

clocks, sixteen red caps, a brush for a cat, and

ten tops. You will see a chess set, a little lamp,

a belt, twenty rocks, and bath stuff.

Do you like Sal's trunk? We can shut the

trunk now.

Starts with *tr*	Ends with *mp*
7. ____trunk____	11. _____
Starts with *cl*	**Ends with *lt***
8. _____	12. _____
Starts with *sh*	**Ends with *sh***
9. _____	13. _____
Starts with *ch*	**Ends with *th***
10. _____	14. _____

Language and Literacy

Words with Blends

A. Name each picture. Write the name.

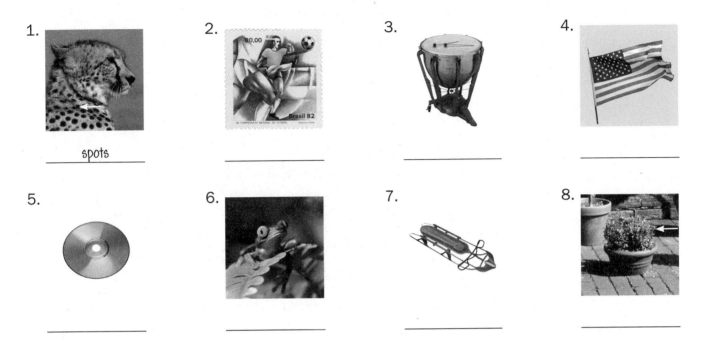

1. __spots__

2. _____

3. _____

4. _____

5. _____

6. _____

7. _____

8. _____

B. Now read the story. Circle the words that go in the chart. Write them in the chart. Write each word one time.

Pack for (Camp)

Jim packs his bag for camp. He needs enough

stuff to last 5 days.

He packs:

• 1 tent and a mat to sleep on

• 2 swim trunks for his swim class

• a belt, 4 snacks, 10 socks, 1 brush,

   and more!

He can smash it all in the bag, but he can not

lift the bag! Jim has to pack two bags for camp.

Starts with *st*	Ends with *st*
9. _____	13. _____
Starts with *tr*	**Ends with *nt***
10. _____	14. _____
Starts with *cl*	**Ends with *mp***
11. _____	15. __Camp__
Starts with *sn*	**Ends with *lt***
12. _____	16. _____

Build Reading Fluency

▶ **Phrasing**

A. When you read, pause between groups of words that go together.

Stan is in / a big rush. //
Stan has three minutes / to catch his plane. //

B. Listen to the story. When you hear a short pause, write a / . When you
hear a long pause, write //.

Rush!

Stan is in a big rush. His plane leaves at 2:00 p.m. The clock says 1:57 p.m. Stan has three minutes to catch his plane. That is not very long! He jumps out of the cab and slams the door. Bang! He drops his bag. All of his things fall out of the bag. Then he drops one more thing—his ticket! A man helps Stan. The first thing he picks up is the bag.

The second thing he picks up is the ticket. The man asks Stan, "When does your plane leave?"

Stan says, "I think it just left without me."

The man looks at Stan's ticket. He grins and tells Stan, "You have enough time. Your plane leaves tomorrow at two.

C. Now read the story to a partner. Read groups of words together. Pause
when you see a /.

Name _____

I Don't Want This Food!

▶ **Contractions with *not***

A. When you make a contraction, you join two words together.

is + not = isn't	do + not = don't
are + not = aren't	does + not = doesn't

Use these contractions in negative sentences.

The food on the plane **isn't** very good.
The cookies **aren't** big.
The cake **doesn't** have nuts.
I **don't** want anything to eat.

B. Read each sentence. Change the underlined words to a contraction. Then complete the new sentence.

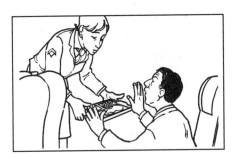

1. He <u>is not</u> happy.
   He ___isn't___ happy.

2. He does not like the food.
   He _____ like the food.

3. She <u>does not</u> eat the cake.
   She _____ eat the cake.

4. The cake <u>is not</u> sweet.
   The cake _____ sweet.

5. They <u>do not</u> want to eat.
   They _____ want to eat.

6. They <u>are not</u> hungry.
   They _____ hungry.

Learn Key Vocabulary

Name _____

The Mighty Maya: Key Vocabulary

A. Study each word. Circle a number to rate how well you know it. Then complete the chart.

Rating Scale	**1** I have never seen this word before.	**2** I am not sure of the word's meaning.	**3** I know this word and can teach the word's meaning to someone else.

▲ This building was made **thousands** of years ago.

Key Words	Check Understanding	Deepen Understanding
❶ **city** (**si**-tē) *noun* **Rating:** 1 2 3	A **city** is very small with few people. Yes No	What city is close to you? _____ _____ _____ _____
❷ **hundreds** (**hun**-dridz) *noun* **Rating:** 1 2 3	An hour has **hundreds** of minutes. Yes No	Name a place where you can see hundreds of people. _____ _____ _____ _____
❸ **population** (pop-yū-**lā**-shun) *noun* **Rating:** 1 2 3	**Population** tells how many people live in one area. Yes No	Name a state with a big population. _____ _____ _____ _____

Key Vocabulary, continued

These **two** men are Mayan. ▶

Key Words	Check Understanding	Deepen Understanding
❹ **thousands** (**thou**-zundz) *noun* **Rating:** 1 2 3	Texas has **thousands** of people. **Yes** **No**	Name a number in the thousands. _____ _____ _____ _____
❺ **two** (tū) *adjective* **Rating:** 1 2 3	A bike has **two** wheels. **Yes** **No**	Name two different holidays. _____ _____ _____ _____

B. Use at least two of the Key Vocabulary words. Describe the population of your class. Is it large or small?

_____

_____

_____

Writing Project

Name _____

Plan and Write

1. What country will you research? _____

2. What do you want to know? Make a list.

   _____   _____

   _____   _____

   _____   _____

3. Choose your focus. Check three items.

4. Turn your list into questions. Write the questions. Research in books or on the
   Internet to find the answers to your questions. Write your answers. Draw a map
   of your country in the box at the top.

Facts About _____

- How large is _____

  The country of _____

  is _____

- What is the _____

  _____

  _____

  _____

- What is _____

  _____

  _____

  _____

A map of _____

Check Your Work

▶ Capitalization and End Marks

Read the fact sheet. Fix capital letters and add end punctuation as needed.
Mark your changes. Then write the questions and answers correctly.

Mark Your Changes

∧ Add.

≡ Capitalize.

Facts About Mexico

A map of Mexico

- How large is mexico

_____

mexico is about 742,485 square miles.

_____

- What is the population of mexico?

_____

The population of Mexico is 108,700,891.

_____

- What is the longest river in mexico

_____

The rio grande is the longest river in Mexico.

_____

- What is the population of the capital city of mexico

_____

The capital city is Mexico city. The population of mexico city is 19,013,000.

_____

Mind Map

Use the mind map to show how to find out about your town or city. As you read the selections in this unit, add new ideas for ways to learn about a city.

How to Find Out About Your City

Language Development

Where Is It?

▶ **Language: Ask For and Give Information**

▶ **Vocabulary: Location Words**

A. Study the places.

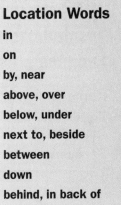

Location Words

in

on

by, near

above, over

below, under

next to, beside

between

down

behind, in back of

B. Complete each sentence. Tell where the places are. Use location words.

1. The pet shop is _____ on _____ the corner.

2. You can get dog food _____ the pet shop.

3. The toy store is _____ the café.

4. The toy store is _____ the music store and the market.

5. You go _____ the stairs to get from the market to the bakery.

6. The market is _____ the bakery.

7. The café is _____ the bakery.

8. There are two plants _____ the café.

9. There is someone _____ the door to the bakery.

10. The theater is _____ the pet shop.

Language Development

Name _____

Things in the Neighborhood

▶ **Vocabulary: Neighborhood**

▶ **Language: Ask For and Give Information**

A. Name each place. Then name something you see there. Use words from the box.

| intersection | post office | bus station | store | bus | parking lot | mailbox | stop sign |

1.

bus

bus station

2.

3.

4.

B. Answer each question. Use a complete sentence.

5. What happens at the bus station?

   People wait for the bus.

6. What happens at the intersection?

   _____

7. What happens at the store?

   _____

8. What happens at the post office?

   _____

© NGSP & HB

Language Development

On My Street

▶ Grammar: Regular Past Tense Verbs

A verb changes to show the past tense.

She **cooks** the food.

She **cooked** the food.

Look at each picture. Read the sentence. Circle the correct verb.

1.

They _____ **play / (played)** _____ soccer.

2.

She _____ **parks / parked** _____ her car.

3.

He _____ **opens / opened** _____ the bag of chips.

4.

She _____ **adds / added** _____ flowers to the garden.

5.

He _____ **cleans / cleaned** _____ the car.

6.

They _____ **help / helped** _____ win the game.

Language Development

We Visited the Zoo

▶ **Regular Past Tense Verbs**

You can add *–ed* to many verbs to tell about things that happened in the past.

We **wanted** to go to the city zoo.

I **asked** Mom to take us there.

Complete each sentence. Add the past tense of the verb in dark type.

1. We _____walked_____ around the zoo.
   (walk)

2. Sam _____ the young lions.
   (watch)

3. They _____ so big!
   (look)

4. Tara _____ away from them!
   (stay)

5. I _____ to see the monkeys.
   (ask)

6. They _____ all around.
   (jump)

7. One monkey _____ a ball.
   (toss)

8. We _____ to them yell!
   (listen)

9. Mom _____ .
   (laugh)

10. We all _____ our visit.
    (enjoy)

Identify Details

▶ **Sum It Up**

A. Read what Sergio did in his neighborhood. Make a detail chart to show what he did and when he did it. The first row in the chart has been filled in for you.

> ### Sergio's Busy Week
>
> Sergio has many nice neighbors. He spent a lot of time this week helping them after school. On Monday, Sergio shopped for dog treats. Then he walked Mrs. Perez's dog. On Tuesday, he mowed the grass for Mr. Mendez. He read the paper to Mr. Mendez, too. On Wednesday, Sergio carried groceries for Mrs. Gold. Then he stacked groceries on her kitchen shelves. On Thursday, Sergio watched Mrs. Lee's twin boys. On Friday, Sergio played baseball after school. All the neighbors went to the game and cheered for him!

Detail Chart

Day	Events
Monday	shopped for dog treats, walked dog

B. Imagine that you are one of Sergio's neighbors. Write a thank-you note to thank him for helping you.

Dear Sergio,

Thank you for _____

_____

_____

Your neighbor,

_____

High Frequency Words, Part 1

A. Read each word. Then write it.

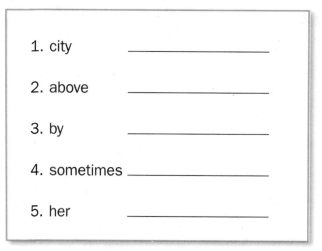

1. city _____
2. above _____
3. by _____
4. sometimes _____
5. her _____

B. Read each sentence. Find the new words in the box. Write the words on the lines.

6. These 2 words end with **y**.

_____city_____   _____

7. These 2 words are location words.

_____   _____

8. This word rhymes with **my**.

_____

9. This word has 2 smaller words in it.

_____

10. This word has **er**.

_____

Language and Literacy

High Frequency Words, Part 2

A. Read each word. Then write it.

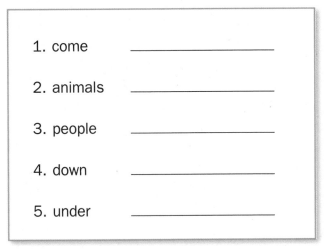

1. come _____

2. animals _____

3. people _____

4. down _____

5. under _____

B. Read each sentence. Find the new words in the box. Write the words on the lines.

6. This word starts with **c**.

_____ come _____

7. These 2 words name living things.

_____   _____

8. These 2 words are location words.

_____   _____

9. These 2 words end with **e**.

_____   _____

10. This word has **er**.

_____

Words with Long and Short Vowels

A. Name each picture. Read the two words. Circle the word that names the picture.

1.

face / fact

2.

hi / hill

3.

be / bell

4.

wet / we

B. Now read the story. Circle the words with long e. Then circle the words with short e. Write them in the chart. Write each word one time.

(We) Like to Swim!

We like to swim. But I do not like to (get) wet! The pool is near my home. I walk there with Kim. She is my friend. We can be in the water until the bell rings. Then we have to get out. As we wait, I get dry. When they let us back in the pool, I get wet again! I like to swim so much that I do not mind if I get wet. Kim bet me I would like swimming more if I could stay dry, but I cannot do that! She is funny.

Words with long e	Words with short e
5. _____we_____	9. _____get_____
6. _____	10. _____
7. _____	11. _____
8. _____	12. _____
	13. _____
	14. _____
	15. _____

Words with Long and Short Vowels

A. Name each picture. Read the two words. Circle the word that names the picture.

1.

he / hen

2.

he / help

3.

hi / hit

4.

be / bell

B. Now read the story. Circle the words with long e. Then circle the words with short e. Write them in the chart. Write each word one time.

At Home in the City

I like my home in the city. On Saturdays, Sal and I (help) at the library. (He) sits at the desk. I show the kids good books. Then I let them look around without me. At 12:00, we are done. Sometimes we stop for lunch. Then we go home. We walk down Grand Road. The city is so great! We can be home in two minutes.

Words with long e	Words with short e
5. ___he___	9. ___help___
6. _____	10. _____
7. _____	11. _____
8. _____	12. _____
	13. _____

Multisyllabic Words

A. Read each word. Write how many syllables it has.

1. pool

_____ l _____

2. nickel

_____

3. moon

_____

4. garden

_____

5. basket

_____

6. napkin

_____

7. screw

_____

8. broom

_____

B. Now read the story. Circle the words with two syllables. Write each word in the chart. Then write the syllables.

Hunting a Pumpkin

We went to find a pumpkin at the farm. We wanted the biggest one in the field. My sister helped me look. We saw a lot of pumpkins. We also saw a snake! My mom was calling to us. The farmer told us to look in the far corner of the field. There we saw the biggest pumpkin in the whole field! Next to it was a small one. We could not carry the big pumpkin, so we picked the small one.

	Word	Syllable	
9.	hunting	hunt	ing
10.			
11.			
12.			
13.			
14.			
15.			
16.			
17.			
18.			

Multisyllabic Words

A. Read each word. Write how many syllables it has.

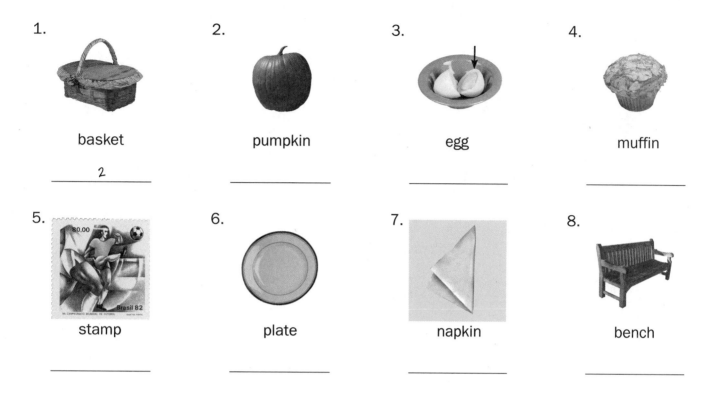

1.

basket

_____2_____

2.

pumpkin

_____

3.

egg

_____

4.

muffin

_____

5.

stamp

_____

6.

plate

_____

7.

napkin

_____

8.

bench

_____

B. Now read the story. Circle the words with two syllables. Write each word in the chart. Then write the syllables.

A (Picnic) in the Park

Jan and Chun go on a picnic. Jan packs lunch in a basket. Chun grabs a blanket. Then they put on their helmets and hop on their bikes. They ride through a tunnel, then up to Elm Road. They watch out for traffic. At the park, they see lots of children. Chun puts the blanket on the grass, and they sit down. "Let's eat," Jan says. "Do you want a sandwich?"

Word	Syllable	
9. _____picnic_____	pic	nic
10. _____	_____	_____
11. _____	_____	_____
12. _____	_____	_____
13. _____	_____	_____
14. _____	_____	_____
15. _____	_____	_____
16. _____	_____	_____

Build Reading Fluency

▶ Expression

A. Some sentences tell something. Other sentences show strong feeling.

This sentence tells something. It ends with a period.

Jo works at the City Animal Hospital **.**

This sentence shows a strong feeling. It ends with an exclamation mark.

He is so soft **!**

B. Listen to the different kinds of sentences.

Meet Jo

Jo works at the City Animal Hospital. I asked her to tell me about what she does at her job.

I have a great job. I love to help the animals. Look. This cat got hit by traffic. It is so sad when that happens. I had to make her a special bed. She has to lie down a lot.

This is Samson. Samson has a bad rash. He has this thing around his neck so he can't bite the skin under it. Sometimes we play catch.

He needs to run a lot. He likes to run down the hill to the park. We rest under the trees. I like to look at the sky above us as Samson sleeps.

This rabbit is Velvet. I like to brush him. He is so soft! Velvet had to get his shots. He needs to rest for a day or two. Then he will go home.

So, that is my job. I help hundreds of animals. It is great to see them get well. I miss them when people come to take them home.

C. Now read the sentences to a partner. See how your reading improves!

They're from My Neighborhood

▶ Pronoun-Verb Contractions

A. You can put a pronoun and a verb together to form a contraction.

I + am = I'm	**I'm** on the sidewalk.
you + are = you're	**You're** slow.
he + is = he's she + is = she's it + is = it's	**It's** a sunny day.
we + are = we're	**We're** glad to be together.
they + are = they're	**They're** in the park.

B. Combine the words in dark type to make a contraction. Use the contraction to complete the sentence.

1. Sam and Kim are Mia's friends. _____They're_____ her neighbors.
   (They are)

2. Mia walks the dogs for Sam and Kim. _____ happy to do it.
   (She is)

3. One dog stops to rest. _____ a small dog.
   (He is)

4. Mia laughs at the dog. "_____ slow, Biff."
   (You are)

5. "You can rest, Biff. _____ not in a hurry."
   (We are)

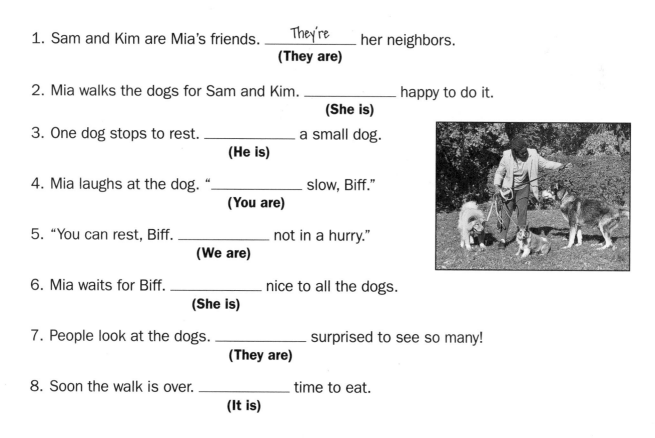

6. Mia waits for Biff. _____ nice to all the dogs.
   (She is)

7. People look at the dogs. _____ surprised to see so many!
   (They are)

8. Soon the walk is over. _____ time to eat.
   (It is)

Learn Key Vocabulary

San Francisco: Key Vocabulary

A. Study each word. Circle a number to rate how well you know it.
Then complete the chart.

Rating Scale	**1** I have never seen this word before.	**2** I am not sure of the word's meaning.	**3** I know this word and can teach the word's meaning to someone else.

▲ The city of San Francisco has many tall **buildings**.

Key Words	Check Understanding	Deepen Understanding
❶ buildings (**bil**-dings) *noun* **Rating:** 1 2 3	Houses are **buildings**. **Yes** **No**	What makes buildings look good? _____ _____ _____ _____
❷ live (**liv**) *verb* **Rating:** 1 2 3	Many people **live** in cities. **Yes** **No**	Where would you like to live? _____ _____ _____ _____
❸ neighborhood (**nā**-bor-hood) *noun* **Rating:** 1 2 3	A **neighborhood** is made up of homes and shops. **Yes** **No**	Describe your neighborhood. _____ _____ _____ _____

Name _____

San Francisco was once a small **town** with only a few **buildings** like this one. ▶

Key Words	Check Understanding	Deepen Understanding
❹ store (stor) *noun* **Rating:** 1 2 3	You can buy things at a **store**. **Yes** **No**	Describe a store near you. _____ _____ _____ _____
❺ town (toun) *noun* **Rating:** 1 2 3	A **town** and a city are the same size. **Yes** **No**	Tell about a town that you have visited. _____ _____ _____ _____

B. Use at least two of the Key Vocabulary words. Tell what makes your neighborhood special.

_____

_____

_____

Writing Project

Plan and Write

1. Think about things you did last week. Complete the chart.

Day	Events	Place
Monday		
Tuesday		
Wednesday		
Thursday		
Friday		
Saturday		
Sunday		

2. Use your notes to write a journal page. Use past tense verbs.

Last Monday, I _____

On Tuesday, _____

On Wednesday, _____

On Thursday, _____

On Friday, _____

On Saturday, _____

On Sunday, _____

Check Your Work

▶ Capitalization and End Marks

Read this journal page. Fix capital letters and add end punctuation as needed. Mark your changes. Then write each sentence correctly.

Mark Your Changes

∧ Add.

≡ Capitalize.

Last monday, i played baseball in the park

_____

On tuesday, I looked for books in the library

_____

On wednesday, i shopped at the mall

_____

On Thursday, i went to dinner in a restaurant

_____

On friday, I visited my friend at her house

_____

On saturday, I cleaned my bedroom

_____

On sunday, i cooked breakfast in my kitchen

_____

Mind Map

Use the mind map to show what you know about family life. As you read the selections in this unit, add new ideas you learn about the people, places, and events that are part of family life.

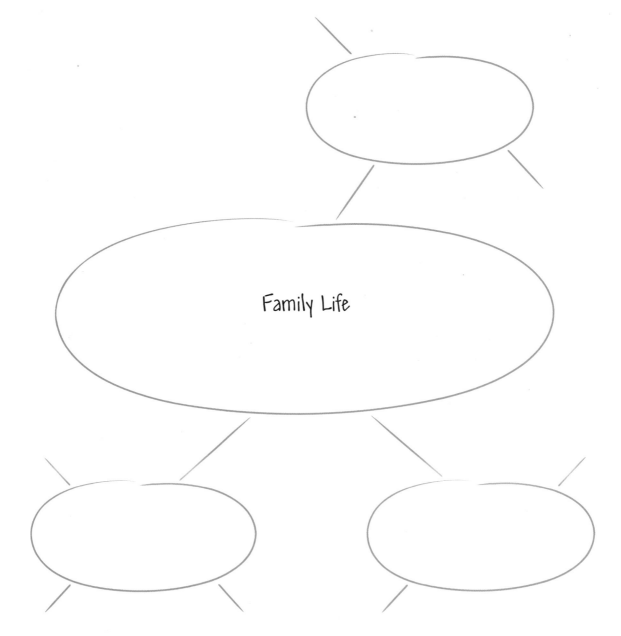

Family Life

Language Development

Meet Lin's Family

▶ **Language: Give Information**

▶ **Vocabulary: Family**

A. Use family words to tell about Lin's family tree. Then answer the question below.

Family Words

grandfather	brother
grandmother	sister
father	uncle
mother	aunt

grandfather

Lin

Lin's Family Tree

B. How many people are in Lin's family? _____ of them together make up Lin's family tree.

Language Development

I Have a Great Family

▶ **Grammar: Present Tense Verbs:** *Have* **and** *Has*

Use *have* with *I*, *you*, *we*, and *they*. Use *has* with *he*, *she*, or *it*.

Hi. I'm Rita. **I have** a sister. We **have** a new brother. He **has** a room. It **has** toys in it.

Complete each sentence. Use *have* or *has*.

1.

"I ____have____ an aunt."

"She _____ a dog."

2.

"We _____ a small house."

"The house _____ trees around it."

3.

He _____ a sister.

They _____ fun together.

4.

He _____ an uncle.

His uncle _____ a big bike.

Name _____

What Is in Each Room?

▶ **Vocabulary: Household Objects**

▶ **Language: Ask and Answer Questions**

A. Name the things in each room. Use words from the box.

bathtub	bed	lamp	oven
couch	dresser	sink	shower
stove	rug	refrigerator	door

dresser

B. Answer each question. Use a complete sentence.

1. Where is the couch?   The couch is in the living room. _____

2. Where is the dresser? _____

3. Where is the oven? _____

C. Write two questions. Ask about two things in the rooms above.

4. _____

5. _____

Identify Details that Support a Main Idea

▶ **Sum It Up**

Read the following article. Read the main idea. Write the important ideas in the Main Idea Diagram.

Chinese Family Traditions

Families that lived a long time ago in China had many traditions. Grandparents lived with one of their children and helped take care of the grandchildren. Then as the grandparents got older, their children and grandchildren took care of them. Babies were often named after family members from older generations. Holidays such as the Chinese New Year were celebrated with family members. Younger people showed respect to older people. The older people gave gifts to the youngsters. When it was time to marry, the parents or grandparents chose a husband or wife for their child. The Chinese believed that their traditions made strong families.

Families that lived a long time ago in China had many traditions.

High Frequency Words, Part 1

A. Read each word. Then write it.

1. family   _____

2. together   _____

3. other   _____

4. really   _____

5. father   _____

B. Read the clue. Write the word in the chart. Then write the word again in the sentence.

What to Look For	Word	Sentence
6. begins with **fam**	f a m i l y	My ___family___ loves games.
7. begins with **to**	__ __ __ __ __ __ __ __	We like to be _____ .
8. begins with **o**	__ __ __ __ __	We do _____ things, too.
9. begins with **r**	__ __ __ __ __ __	We have a _____ big family.
10. means "dad"	__ __ __ __ __ __	My _____ is an artist.

High Frequency Words, Part 2

A. Read each word. Then write it.

1. mother _____

2. our _____

3. watch _____

4. eyes _____

5. head _____

B. Read the clue. Write the word in the chart. Then write the word again in the sentence.

What to Look For	Word	Sentence
6. means "mom"	m o t h e r	My ___mother___ is a writer.
7. has 3 letters	__ __ __	Friday is _____ game night.
8. ends with **tch**	__ __ __ __ __	Sometimes we _____ TV.
9. has **yes** in it	__ __ __ __	I use my _____ to do puzzles.
10. rhymes with **bed**	__ __ __ __	I think with my _____ .

Words with Long Vowels: *a_e, o_e*

A. Name each picture. Write the name.

1. ____tape____

2. _____

3. _____

4. _____

5. _____

6. _____

7. _____

8. _____

B. Now read the story. Circle the words with long *a* or long *o*. Write them in the chart. Write each word one time.

Trouble at the (Lake)

Our home is close to a lake. The lake is big. Sometimes it has big waves.

One day I take a ride and get to the lake. I gaze out. Those waves are big! I see a boy in trouble. A man comes by and spots the boy. He jumps into the water and swims out with big strokes. I shut my eyes and hope he can save the boy. And he does!

I spoke to the man. "That was very brave!" I said.

9. ____Lake____	15. _____
10. _____	16. _____
11. _____	17. _____
12. _____	18. _____
13. _____	19. _____
14. _____	20. _____

Language and Literacy

Words with Long Vowels

A. Name each picture. Write the name.

1.

_____cape_____

2.

_____

3.

_____

4.

_____

5.

_____

6.

_____

7.

_____

8.

_____

B. Now read the story. Circle the words with long *a, i, o,* or *u.* Write them in the chart. Write each word one time.

Fun with Bill

My brother Bill(drives)a truck all around the state. When he is home, he makes life fun.

Once he put together kites for all the kids in the family. Bill had to use long, thin tubes for the frames. The wings were cloth from a torn robe. "The kites are cute," he said, "but I hope we can get them up in the air!"

9. _____	15. _____
10. _____	16. _____
11. _____	17. _____
12. ___drives___	18. _____
13. _____	19. _____
14. _____	20. _____

Words with Short and Long Vowels

A. Name each picture. Read the two words. Circle the word that names the picture.

1.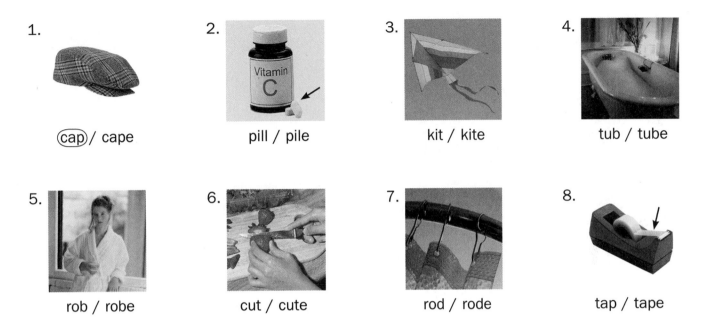
(cap)/ cape

2.
pill / pile

3.
kit / kite

4.
tub / tube

5.
rob / robe

6.
cut / cute

7.
rod / rode

8.
tap / tape

B. Now read the story. Circle the words with long *o* or long *i*. Underline the words with short *o* or short *i*. Write them in the chart. Write each word one time.

A Busy (Home)

We are really busy. Here <u>is</u> what a day is like. Mom drives to the pet shop. She must be there by three. The shop closes at three. Then Mom stops to get us snacks to eat. Dad helps me fix my bike, and then we scrub the stove. Pam has to watch the baby next door. At the end of the day, we like to sit down and rest. That is when we can all be together again.

9. _____Home_____	15. _____
10. _____	16. _____
11. _____	17. _____
12. _____	18. _____
13. _____	19. _____
14. _____	20. _____

Plurals

A. Name each picture. Read the two words. Circle the word that names the picture.

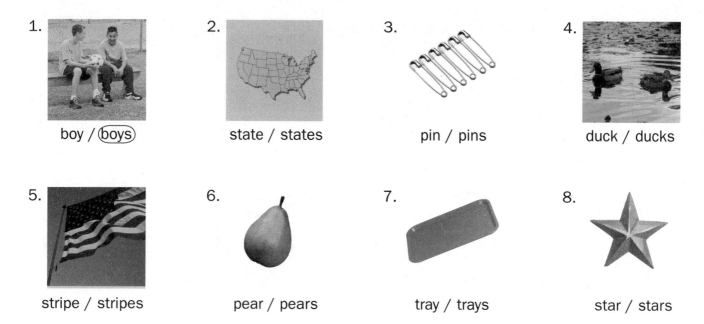

1. boy / (boys)

2. state / states

3. pin / pins

4. duck / ducks

5. stripe / stripes

6. pear / pears

7. tray / trays

8. star / stars

B. Now read the story. Circle the words that name more than one thing. Write them in the chart. Write each word one time.

(Parades) in the City

Our city has many parades for kids. The parades are a lot of fun. Girls and boys pass by in bands. They play drums and trumpets and other things. Girls do tricks with batons. We see costumes with a lot of colors. We see many pets, too. Boys and girls pass by with their dogs, cats, and snakes. Parents stand on the sidewalk and clap. They like to see the kids.

Plurals	
9. _____parades_____	18. _____
10. _____	19. _____
11. _____	20. _____
12. _____	21. _____
13. _____	22. _____
14. _____	23. _____
15. _____	24. _____
16. _____	25. _____
17. _____	

Name _____

Build Reading Fluency

▶ **Phrasing**

A. When you read, pause between groups of words that go together.

In Nicaragua, / my family made / big puppets to sell. //
We made the arms / from long tubes. //

B. Listen to the story. When you hear a short pause, write a / . When you hear a long pause, write //.

Example: In Nicaragua, / my family made / big puppets to sell.//

When We Came to Wisconsin

Hi. My name is Pablo Soto. My mother's name is Sandra. We are from Nicaragua.

In Nicaragua, our family made big puppets to sell. The name of one puppet that we made is *La Gigantona*. We made the head of this puppet with paper and paste. We made the eyes of the puppet really big, with long, thick lashes. We made the arms from long tubes. They swing from side to side. We put a white robe, a cute hat, and other things on the puppet. People like to watch this big puppet in parades.

C. Now read the story to a partner. Use the marks you made to read groups of words together.

Language and Literacy

Name _____

New Neighbors

▶ Plural Nouns

A. A noun names a person, place, or thing.

A singular noun names one thing.

box

A plural noun names more than one thing.

boxes

Study these rules for forming plurals.

To make most nouns plural, just add **-s**.	boy boys	girl girls	book books
If the noun ends in **x, ch, sh, s,** or **z,** add **-es**.	box boxes	dish dishes	glass glasses
Some nouns change in different ways.	man men	woman women	child children

B. Complete each sentence. Use the plural form of the word in dark type.

1. Two ___**women**___ bring food.
   (woman)

2. There are many _____ to unpack.
   (box)

3. Mrs. Lee finds the _____ .
   (dish)

4. Then she finds the _____ .
   (cup)

5. They eat their _____ .
   (lunch)

6. Mrs. Lee has two new _____ .
   (friend)

Learn Key Vocabulary

The Family Reunion: Key Vocabulary

A. Study each word. Circle a number to rate how well you know it. Then complete the chart.

▲ This **family** is **together** at a party.

Rating Scale	**1** I have never seen this word before.	**2** I am not sure of the word's meaning.	**3** I know this word and can teach the word's meaning to someone else.

Key Words	Check Understanding	Deepen Understanding
❶ cousins (**ku**-zinz) *noun* **Rating:** 1 2 3	My **cousins** are my mother's sisters. Yes No	How are cousins related to each other? _____ _____ _____ _____
❷ family (**fa**-mu-lē) *noun* **Rating:** 1 2 3	A **family** can be big or small. Yes No	Name at least two people in your family. _____ _____ _____ _____
❸ grandchildren (**grand**-chil-drun) *noun* **Rating:** 1 2 3	Grandparents can have many **grandchildren**. Yes No	Tell about the grandchildren in your family. _____ _____ _____ _____

Name _____

These **parents** like to play music with their children. ▶

Key Words	Check Understanding	Deepen Understanding
❹ **parents** (**pair**-ents) *noun* **Rating:**　1　2　3	Your brother and sister are your **parents**. Yes　　　　No	Name something parents do for children. _____ _____ _____ _____
❺ **together** (tu-ge-thur) *adverb* **Rating:**　1　2　3	Children often play **together**. Yes　　　　No	What do you and your family do together? _____ _____ _____ _____

B. Use at least two of the Key Vocabulary words. Explain why it is important for family and friends to be together.

_____

_____

_____

Writing Project

Plan and Write

1. Choose two people to write about. Write their names in the first column. Then fill in the chart.

Who?	What the Person Likes	What the Person Does	Where	Something Special About the Person

2. Write a title and your name.

3. Write 3 complete sentences about each person. Tell
   - what the person **likes**
   - what the person **has** and **where** it is
   - **something special** about the person

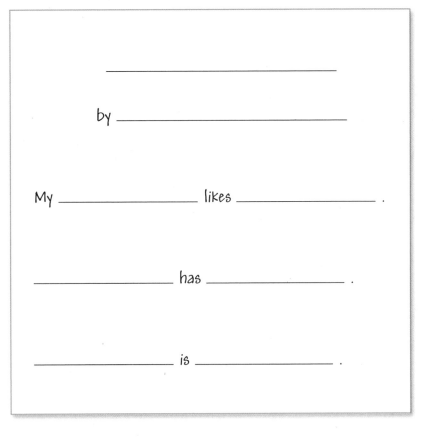

_____

by _____

My _____ likes _____ .

_____ has _____ .

_____ is _____ .

Check Your Work

▶ **Plurals and Details**

Read the descriptions. Fix plural nouns as needed. Mark your changes.
Then write the sentences correctly.

My Family
by Sara Thomas

Uncle Jackson likes trucks. He has two 1969 truck in his garage. He fixes broken car and
truck.

_____

_____

_____

My sister Ramona likes playing in the park. She has a collection of toy car. Ramona
can whistle.

_____

_____

_____

My brother Stuart likes to cook. He has his own pots and pan. He is a cook.

_____

_____

_____

My cousins like to play guitar. They have instrument. They know many song.

_____

_____

_____

Mind Map

Use the mind map to show what you know about the rain forest. As you read the selections in this unit, add new ideas you learn about the plants, animals, and landforms of the rain forest.

Pack Your Bags — for the Rain Forest!

Plants	Animals	Landforms	What to Pack

Give Commands

▶ Language: Give and Carry Out Commands

Commands
A **command** tells you what to do or what not to do.
Pack your bags.
Don't forget.

A. Study the commands.

Wear a jacket.	Get some warm clothes.	Find a seat.
Grab a camera.	Ride the bus.	Pack your bag.
Enjoy the trip!	Take some gloves.	Step on the bus.
Dress for snow.	Don't forget a hat.	Take some film.

B. Write two commands for each picture. Use commands from the box.

1.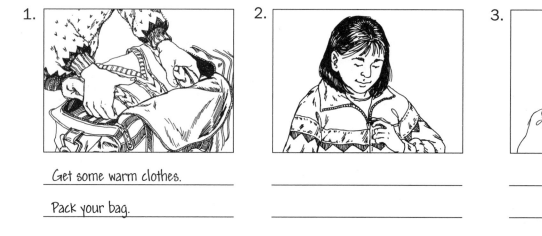

Get some warm clothes.

Pack your bag.

_____

2.

_____

_____

_____

3.

_____

_____

_____

4.

_____

_____

_____

5.

_____

_____

_____

6.

_____

_____

_____

What Do You See?

▶ **Vocabulary: Landforms and Transportation**

▶ **Language: Describe Places**

A. Name the places and things in the picture. Use words from the box.

| ocean | forest | sailboat | airplane | beach | island |

island

| small | tall | hot | dry | fast |

B. Complete each sentence. Describe the picture above. Use adjectives from the box.

1. The island has a forest with _____tall_____ trees.

2. A _____ airplane flies over the island.

3. A _____ sailboat sails on the ocean.

4. The _____ sun shines on the beach.

5. It makes the sand hot and _____ .

Language Development

What Do They Wear?

▶ **Vocabulary: Weather and Clothing**

▶ **Language: Give Information**

A. Name the things to wear. Use words from the box.

sneaker	glove	scarf	bathing suit	sandal	parka

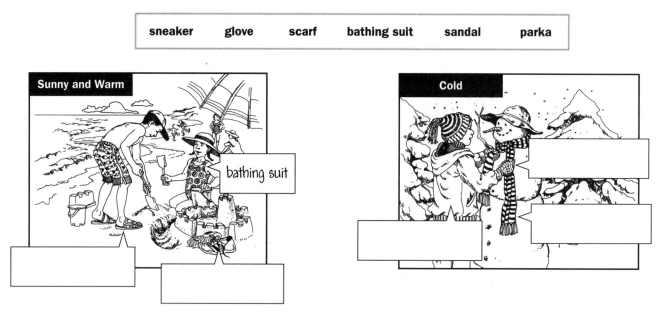

Sunny and Warm

bathing suit

Cold

B. What is the weather like? Tell Brandon and Rachel what clothing to pack.

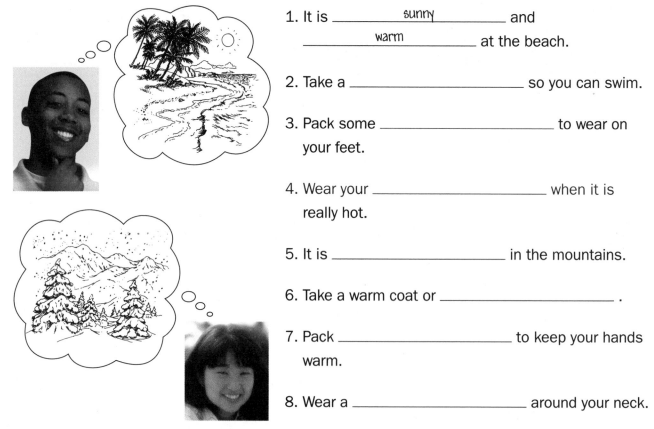

1. It is _____ sunny _____ and _____ warm _____ at the beach.

2. Take a _____ so you can swim.

3. Pack some _____ to wear on your feet.

4. Wear your _____ when it is really hot.

5. It is _____ in the mountains.

6. Take a warm coat or _____ .

7. Pack _____ to keep your hands warm.

8. Wear a _____ around your neck.

Language Development

Yes, You Can!

▶ Grammar: Use the Verb *Can*

Use *can* before another verb to tell what people are able to do.

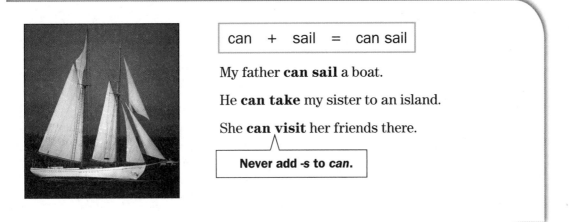

| can | + | sail | = | can sail |

My father **can sail** a boat.

He **can take** my sister to an island.

She **can visit** her friends there.

Never add -s to *can*.

Complete each sentence. Tell what the people in each picture can do. Use *can* and a word from the box.

| work | wear | see | hike | ski | play | plant | swim |

winter   **spring**   **summer**   **fall**

1. In the winter, he _____ can ski _____ in the mountains.

2. In the winter, he _____ in the snow.

3. In the spring, she _____ in the garden.

4. In the spring, she _____ flowers.

5. In the summer, he _____ in the pool.

6. In the summer, he _____ a bathing suit.

7. In the fall, they _____ pretty trees.

8. In the fall, they _____ in the park.

Name _____

Classify Information

▶ **Sum It Up**

A. Think of a place you would like to explore. Write the name in the middle of the concept map below. Then write what you can see there, what the weather is like, and what you would wear.

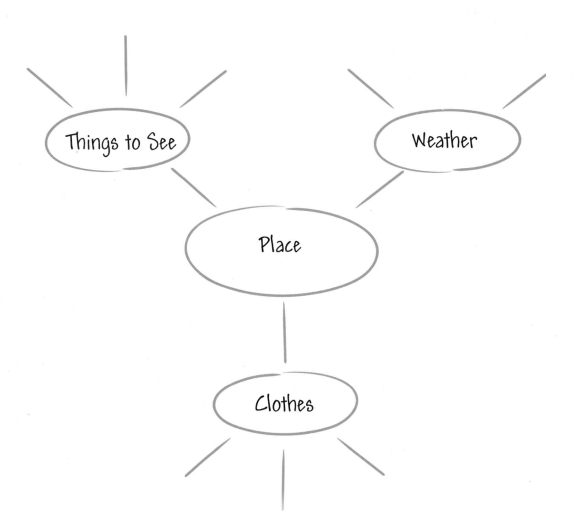

B. Write sentences to describe the place you would like to explore.

_____

_____

_____

_____

High Frequency Words, Part 1

A. Read each word. Then write it.

1. places   _____

2. important   _____

3. world   _____

4. always   _____

5. or   _____

B. Find the new words. Write the words on the lines.

6. These 2 words have a **w**.

_____always_____   _____

C. Work with a partner. Follow the steps.

• Read aloud each new word in the box.

• Your partner writes the words.

• Have your partner read the words to you.

• Now you write the words on the lines below.

• Read the words to your partner.

7. _____

8. _____

9. _____

10. _____

11. _____

Name _____

High Frequency Words, Part 2

A. Read each word. Then write it.

1. river   _____

2. through   _____

3. once   _____

4. water   _____

5. below   _____

B. Find the new words in the box. Write the words on the lines.

6. These 2 words have a **w**.

_____ water _____   _____

C. Work with a partner. Follow the steps.

• Read aloud each new word in the box.

• Your partner writes the words.

• Have your partner read the words to you.

• Now you write the words on the lines below.

• Read the words to your partner.

7. _____

8. _____

9. _____

10. _____

11. _____

Name _____

Words with Long *a*

A. Read each word. Which picture goes with the word? Write its letter.

1. tray _D_   2. stain ___   3. play ___

4. sail ___   5. midday ___   6. train ___

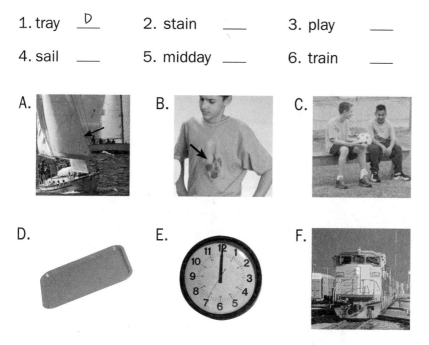

A. B. C.

D. E. F.

B. Now read the story. Circle long *a* words with *ai* and *ay*. Write them in the chart. Write each word one time.

My Grandma's Chair

My grandma has a favorite chair. She (mainly) keeps it upstairs. It has blue and purple flowers in a chain. It is big and soft. When I was little, my grandma let me play in her chair. I would pretend to be an old lady.

My grandma has gray hair, but she likes to do many things. She loves to raise the window shades early in the day. Sometimes, my grandma and I collect daisies. Then she might say, "Now, you may sit in my special chair." I always wait for her to tell me.

7. _mainly_	12. _____
8. _____	13. _____
9. _____	14. _____
10. _____	15. _____
11. _____	16. _____
	17. _____

Words with Long *a*, Long *e*, and Long *o*

A. Read each word. Which picture goes with the word? Write its letter.

1. coast __N__
2. boat ___
3. train ___
4. braid ___
5. road ___
6. seeds ___
7. paints ___
8. feet ___
9. sail ___
10. tree ___
11. tray ___
12. geese ___
13. crow ___
14. seal ___
15. tea ___

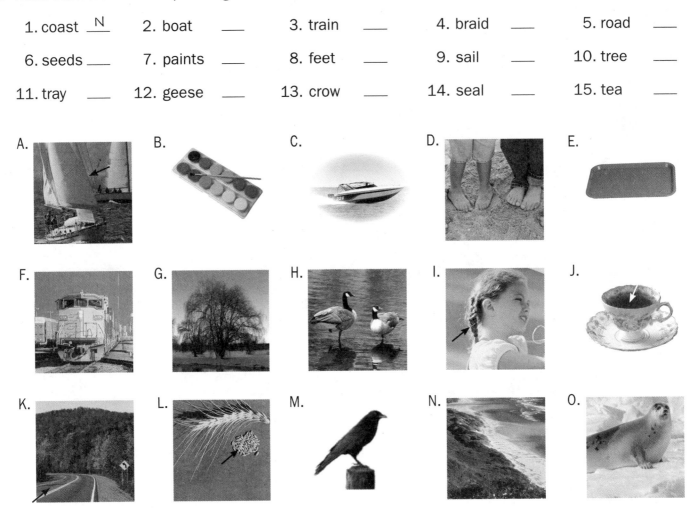

B. Name each picture below. Which words above have the same long vowel sound as the picture name? Write the words on the lines.

16. **Sunday MAY 8**   train ___ / ___ / ___

17. ___ / ___ / ___ / ___

18. ___ / ___

Name _____

Words with Short and Long Vowels

A. Name each picture. Read the two words. Circle the word that names the picture.

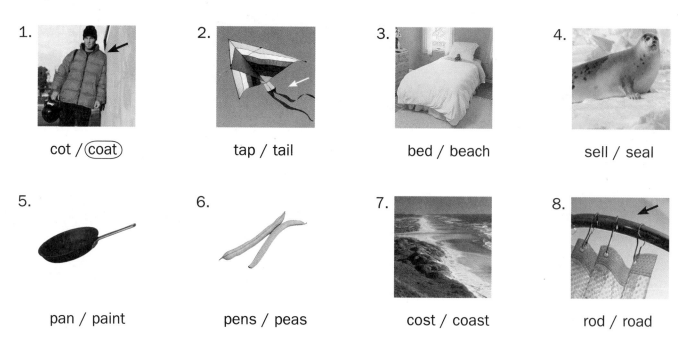

1. cot / (coat)

2. tap / tail

3. bed / beach

4. sell / seal

5. pan / paint

6. pens / peas

7. cost / coast

8. rod / road

B. Now read the story. Circle the words with long *a*. Underline the words with short *a*. Write them in the chart. Write each word one time.

Mom to the Rescue!

Nick (always) goes home to see his mom once a year. He <u>packs</u> his gray bag. What if it rains? Nick gets his coat. What if it's hot? Nick gets his swim trunks. He runs to catch the train, but he forgets his bag! Mom meets Nick in Bay City. She asks, "Where is your bag?" At home, Mom looks through the house. Nick waits. Mom comes back with his old clothes!

9. __always__

10. _____

11. _____

12. _____

13. _____

14. _____

15. __packs__

16. _____

17. _____

18. _____

19. _____

20. _____

Multisyllabic Words

A. Read each word. Write how many syllables it has.

1. weekend
   2

2. crow
   _____

3. rowboat
   _____

4. train
   _____

5. coast
   _____

6. seashell
   _____

7. sunset
   _____

8. stream
   _____

B. Now read the story. Circle the words with two syllables. Write each word in the chart one time. Then write the syllables.

At the Seashore

Dean goes to the seashore on weekends. On wet days, Dean wears his raincoat down to the beach. He hunts for seashells and digs for clams. On warm days, he stays on a sailboat with his dad. They sail from sunrise to sunset. Dean loves his weekends at the seashore.

Word	Syllables	
9. seashore	sea	shore
10.		
11.		
12.		
13.		
14.		
15.		

Build Reading Fluency

▶ **Phrasing**

A. When you read, pause between groups of words that go together.

Stay in your seat / while we move through the water. //
This is an important place / for animals, / too. //

B. Listen to the story. When you hear a short pause, write a / . When you hear a long pause, write //.

Example: Welcome to Black Creek Wetland. // What a great way to spend / a Sunday afternoon. //

Explore a Wetland

Welcome to Black Creek Wetland. What a great way to spend a Sunday afternoon! My name is Jean Clay. I am your guide. Step into the rowboat. Stay in your seat while we move through the water.

Canada has many wetlands. Black Creek Wetland is one of them. A wetland is a low, wet place. Rainwater and many streams or rivers keep it wet. Black Creek is on the shore of Lake Ontario. Plants such as reeds and cattails grow here. This is an important place for animals, too. Ducks and geese lay their eggs here in May.

Sometimes, people drain the water from wetlands. Then they use the land to grow wheat or other crops. Not here. We plan to keep this wetland for the ducks, geese, and other animals.

C. Now read the story to a partner. Read groups of words together. Make a short pause when you see a /. Make a long pause when you see a // .

Language and Literacy

Name _____

Special Places, Special People

▶ **Capitalization: Proper Nouns**

A. A proper noun names one particular person, place, or thing.

A proper noun begins with a <u>capital</u> letter.

name of a person	**Sabrina** helps kids at a summer camp.
name of a special place, a city, or a country	She works at **Camp Bellwood** in **Cloverdale**, **New York**.
name of a month or a day	Camp begins on **Saturday**, **June** 30.

B. Read each sentence. Circle the letters that should be capital letters.

1. Camp (b)ellwood is in (c)loverdale, New York.

2. It is near sutter mountain.

3. Many campers come from boston, massachusetts.

4. They learn to swim at lake bronson.

5. Their teacher is mindy lee.

6. Sabrina and jamal take campers on a hike through the forest.

7. There is a big party at camp on thursday, july 4.

8. On Wednesday, july 10, the campers visit Joe taylor at his farm.

9. The next week, Jamal takes them to niagara Falls.

10. Everyone is sorry when camp ends on friday, august 2.

Learn Key Vocabulary

Name _____

The Water Planet: Key Vocabulary

A. Study each word. Circle a number to rate how well you know it. Then complete the chart.

▲ The **world's surface** is covered by **oceans**.

Rating Scale	**1** I have never seen this word before.	**2** I am not sure of the word's meaning.	**3** I know this word and can teach the word's meaning to someone else.

Key Words	Check Understanding	Deepen Understanding
❶ cold (cōld) *adjective* **Rating:** 1 2 3	Ice and snow are **cold**. Yes No	What happens when you are in a cold place? _____ _____ _____ _____
❷ ocean (ō-shun) *noun* **Rating:** 1 2 3	An **ocean** is smaller than a pond. Yes No	What would you find in the ocean? _____ _____ _____ _____
❸ surface (sur-fes) *noun* **Rating:** 1 2 3	Lakes are on Earth's **surface**. Yes No	Describe Earth's surface in our region. _____ _____ _____ _____

Name _____

The **ocean** near this beach is **warm**. ▶

Key Words	Check Understanding	Deepen Understanding
❹ warm (wôrm) *adjective* **Rating: 1 2 3**	Things freeze in **warm** places. **Yes No**	Name two warm places _____ _____ _____ _____
❺ world (wirld) *noun* **Rating: 1 2 3**	Our **world** has both land and water. **Yes No**	What part of the world do you live in? _____ _____ _____ _____

B. Use at least two of the Key Vocabulary words. Tell how you use water every day.

_____

_____

_____

Writing Project

Plan and Write

1. What place would you like to write about? _____

2. Look for ideas in books, magazines, or on the Internet. Fill in a concept map.

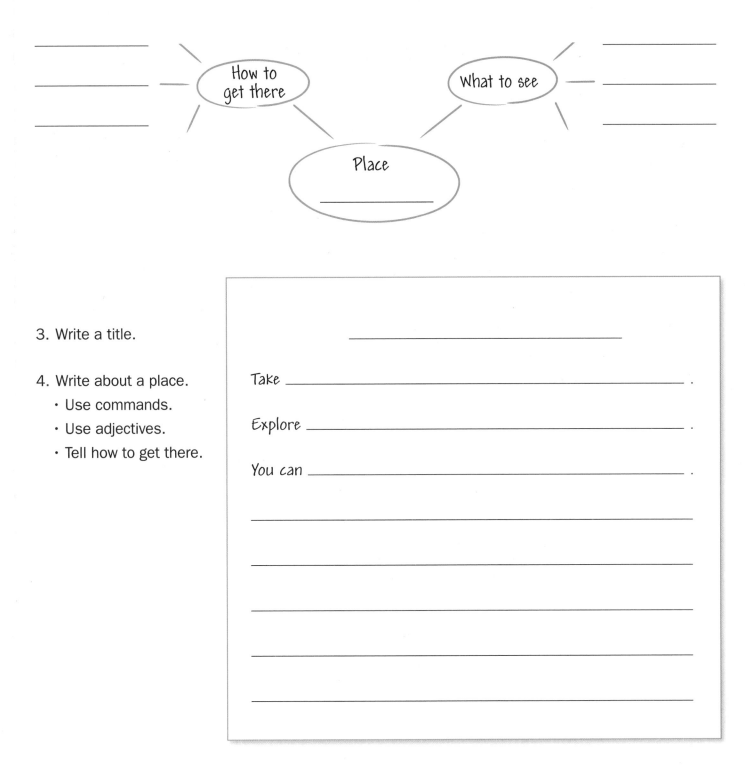

_____
_____

How to get there

What to see

_____
_____

Place

_____

3. Write a title.

_____

4. Write about a place.
   · Use commands.
   · Use adjectives.
   · Tell how to get there.

Take _____ .

Explore _____ .

You can _____ .

_____

_____

_____

_____

5. Copy your sentences onto cards. Attach the cards to a large piece of paper. Add pictures.

Check Your Work

Mark Your Changes

∧ Add.

≡ Capitalize.

▶ Capitalization and Plurals

Read the travel guide. Fix capital letters and plural nouns as needed.
Mark your changes. Then write the paragraph correctly.

Visit Florida Now!

Take a trip to sunny Florida! You can learn about space travel at the kennedy Space Center. You can swim at the white sand beaches in fort myers. You can ride on fun rides at disney world. You can see many alligator in the Everglades. Explore florida! There is so much to see and do!

_____

_____

_____

_____

_____

_____

_____

_____

_____

_____

_____

_____

_____

Mind Map

Use the mind map to show ideas about friends and friendship. As you read the selections in this unit, add new ideas you learn about what friends do together.

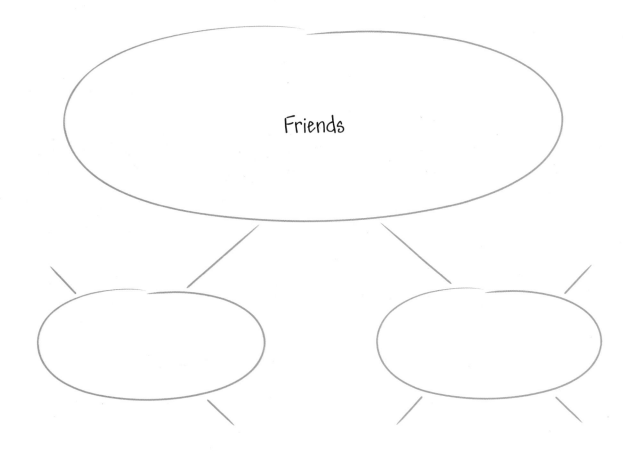

Friends

They Cooked Pizza Together

▶ **Language: Describe Actions**

▶ **Grammar: Past Tense Verbs**

Complete each sentence. Tell what the friends did.
Use a verb from the box.

> **Past Tense Verbs**
> The **past tense** of a verb tells about an action in the past. Many past tense verbs end in **-ed**.
>   Len scratch**ed** his head.

laughed	helped	spilled	rolled
enjoyed	looked	cooked	watched

1.

Miguel ___rolled___ the dough.

Len _____ at the cookbook.

2.

Miguel _____ sauce.

Len _____ about the mess.

3.

Then Len _____ with the dough.

Miguel _____ him.

4.

Finally, the boys _____ the pizza.

They _____ their dinner.

© NGSP & HB

Language Development

How Do They Feel?

▶ **Vocabulary: Feelings**

▶ **Language: Express Feelings**

A. Look at each picture. Tell how the person feels. Use a word from the box.

scared	confused	bored	mad	proud	sad

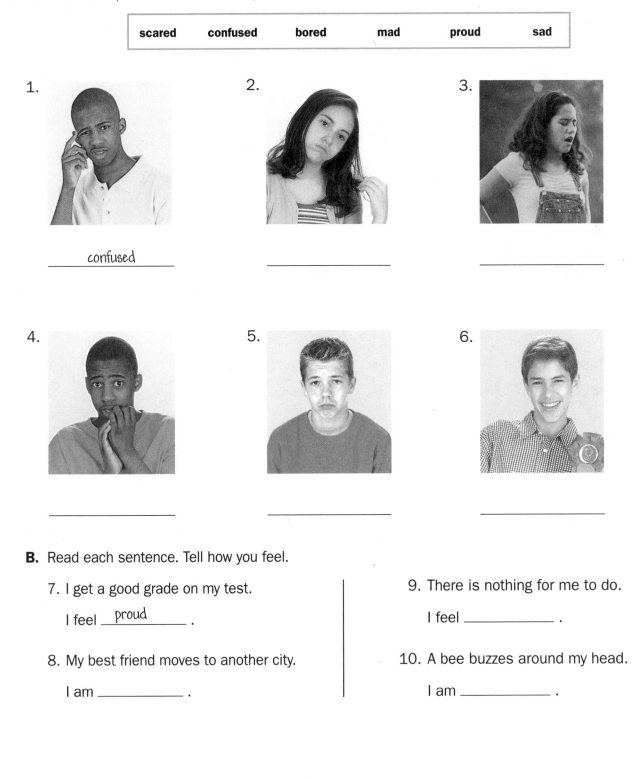

1. _____confused_____

2. _____

3. _____

4. _____

5. _____

6. _____

B. Read each sentence. Tell how you feel.

7. I get a good grade on my test.

   I feel __proud__ .

8. My best friend moves to another city.

   I am _____ .

9. There is nothing for me to do.

   I feel _____ .

10. A bee buzzes around my head.

    I am _____ .

Language Development

It Was Fun to Study Together

▶ **Grammar: Irregular Past Tense Verbs: *Was* and *Were***

Use *was* and *were* to tell about the past.

Pronoun	Verb	Example
I	was	I **was** in the library.
you	were	You **were** by the bookshelf.
he, she, it	was	It **was** warm in the library.
we	were	We **were** not bored.
they	were	They **were** curious about the magazines.

Use ***There was*** for one person or thing.
Use ***There were*** for two or more.

> **There was** a girl beside me.
> **There were** many books to read.

Complete each sentence. Use *was* or *were*.

1. It _____ was _____ 1:30.

2. I _____ with my friends.

3. We _____ in the library.

4. Other students _____ there, too.

5. There _____ a new librarian at the desk.

6. Our table _____ not very big.

7. Carol _____ beside me.

8. There _____ good magazines on the shelf.

9. Mr. Smith _____ glad to answer my questions.

10. It _____ fun to study with my friends.

We Weren't There!

▶ Grammar: Negative Sentences and Contractions with *Not*

There are different ways to build negative sentences in the past tense.

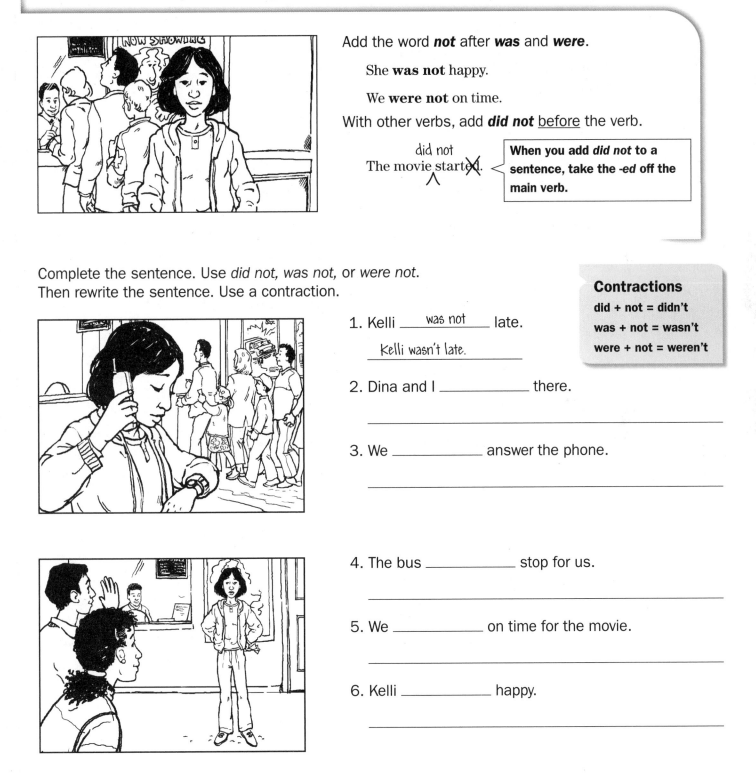

Add the word **not** after **was** and **were**.

She **was not** happy.

We **were not** on time.

With other verbs, add **did not** <u>before</u> the verb.

did not
The movie started.

> **When you add *did not* to a sentence, take the *-ed* off the main verb.**

Complete the sentence. Use *did not, was not,* or *were not*.
Then rewrite the sentence. Use a contraction.

Contractions
did + not = didn't
was + not = wasn't
were + not = weren't

1. Kelli ___was not___ late.

   ___Kelli wasn't late.___

2. Dina and I _____ there.

   _____

3. We _____ answer the phone.

   _____

4. The bus _____ stop for us.

   _____

5. We _____ on time for the movie.

   _____

6. Kelli _____ happy.

   _____

Name _____

Identify Causes and Effects

▶ **Sum It Up**

A. Read the passage. Look for causes and effects. Complete the cause-and-effect chart.

> ### The New Kid
>
> Luis felt nervous as he walked into the lunch room. This was his first day at Greenfield Middle School. He didn't know anyone, so he sat at table by himself.
>
> "How will I ever make friends?" he wondered. "All these people already know each other. They've been in school together for two months." Someone settling into the seat beside him interrupted Luis's thoughts.
>
> "Hi, I'm Eduardo," said the boy. "I just started in this school last week, and I don't know anyone." Suddenly, Luis felt much better. He thought Eduardo might be his first new friend at his new school.

Cause–and–Effect Chart

Causes		Effects
It was Luis's first day at a new school.	→	
	→	
	→	
	→	

B. Write a sentence for each cause and effect in the chart. Use the word *because*.

1. _____

2. _____

3. _____

4. _____

Language and Literacy

High Frequency Words, Part 1

A. Read each word. Then write it.

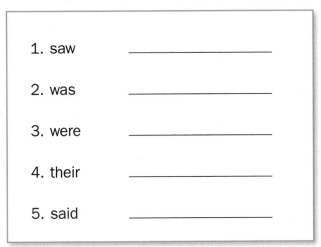

1. saw _____

2. was _____

3. were _____

4. their _____

5. said _____

B. Write the answer to each question. Find the new words in the box. Write the words on the lines.

6. Which 2 words have 3 letters?

_____saw_____   _____

7. Which word rhymes with **her**?

_____

8. Which word has 5 letters?

_____

9. Which word rhymes with **red**?

_____

10. Which word is the past tense of **see**?

_____

High Frequency Words, Part 2

A. Read each word. Then write it.

1. began   _____

2. about   _____

3. dance   _____

4. thought _____

5. again   _____

B. Write the answer to each question. Find the new words in the box. Write the words on the lines.

6. Which word means "started"?

   _____ began _____

7. Which word has 7 letters?

   _____

8. Which 3 words have 2 syllables?

   _____   _____   _____

9. Which 4 words have 5 letters each?

   _____   _____

   _____   _____

10. Which word means "once more"?

    _____

Language and Literacy

Verbs with -ed

A. Read each sentence. Change the word in dark type to tell about the past.

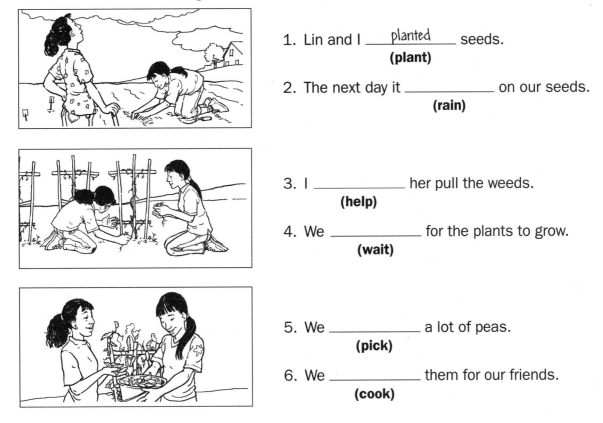

1. Lin and I ___planted___ seeds.
   (plant)

2. The next day it _____ on our seeds.
   (rain)

3. I _____ her pull the weeds.
   (help)

4. We _____ for the plants to grow.
   (wait)

5. We _____ a lot of peas.
   (pick)

6. We _____ them for our friends.
   (cook)

B. Now read the story. Circle the words with -ed. Write each word in the chart one time. Then write the root word.

We (Waited) for the Sun

On Saturday morning it rained. Kim and I waited for the sun. When it peeked through the clouds, we ran to the beach. We saw some birds and hunted for shells by the water. We cleaned the sand off the shells and put them in a box. Then we hunted for tiny crabs in the sand. Kim lifted one crab so we could see it up close.

Word with -ed	Root Word
7. Waited	wait
8. _____	_____
9. _____	_____
10. _____	_____
11. _____	_____
12. _____	_____

Language and Literacy

Verbs with -ed

A. Read each sentence. Change the word in dark type to tell about the past.

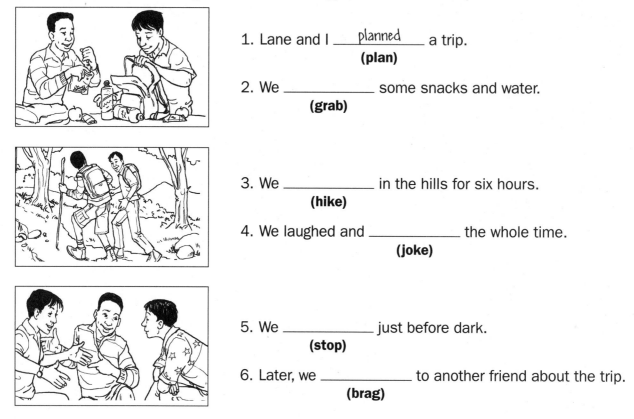

1. Lane and I ___planned___ a trip.
   (plan)

2. We _____ some snacks and water.
   (grab)

3. We _____ in the hills for six hours.
   (hike)

4. We laughed and _____ the whole time.
   (joke)

5. We _____ just before dark.
   (stop)

6. Later, we _____ to another friend about the trip.
   (brag)

B. Now read the story. Circle the words with *-ed*. Write each word in the chart one time. Then write the root word.

With a Friend

Ben's feet (dragged) as he jogged in the park.

Sometimes he hated to jog by himself. He sat

down on a bench to rest. Just then his friend

Matt jogged by and waved.

"Matt!" Ben said. "Wait for me!" He hopped

up and ran to catch up with Matt. He smiled

as they ran side by side. It was more fun to jog

with a friend!

Word with *-ed*	Root Word
7. dragged	drag
8. _____	_____
9. _____	_____
10. _____	_____
11. _____	_____
12. _____	_____

Build Reading Fluency

▶ **Phrasing**

A. When you read, pause between groups of words that go together.

She looked at the clock / above the stove. //
"Veronica has ten more seconds to get
   here," / she said. //

B. Listen to the story. When you hear a short pause, write a / .
When you hear a long pause, write //.

Example: Eva was mad. //She tapped her foot. // She looked at the clock / above the stove. //

Eva's Lesson

Eva was mad. She tapped her foot.

She looked at the clock above the stove.

"Veronica has ten more seconds to get here,"

she said. Eva waited and waited. Veronica

was always late.

They had planned to talk about their dance

for the school show. Eva thought Veronica

was not very good. She thought Veronica

needed a lot of help.

While she waited, Eva played the CD for

their dance. She clapped her hands and

kicked to the beat. She began to sing. She

kicked again. This time, she kicked too high.

She slipped and landed on the rug! Just then,

Veronica peeked in the kitchen window. She

saw Eva and rushed to help her. Eva smiled

and rubbed her leg. "I thought you were the

one who needed help. Now I know I was the

one," she joked.

C. Now read the story to a partner. Read groups of words together. Make a
short pause when you see a /. Make a long pause when you see //.

Meg's Friends

▶ **Possessive Nouns**

A. Some nouns show ownership. They end in 's.

Meg's best friend is Helen. Helen's family lives next door. Helen has a brother. Her brother's name is Fred.

B. Complete each sentence. Add 's to the word in dark print.

1. ___Meg's___ favorite sport is tennis.
   (Meg)

2. Her _____ favorite game is tennis, too.
   (friend)

3. Meg uses her _____ racket to play tennis.
   (dad)

4. Helen borrows her _____ racket.
   (brother)

5. _____ racket is new.
   (Fred)

6. _____ mom and dad take the girls
   (Helen)
   to the park.

7. They play tennis in the _____ park.
   (city)

8. Then _____ brother brings the girls home.
   (Helen)

Learn Key Vocabulary

Hand in Hand: Key Vocabulary

A. Study each word. Circle a number to rate how well
you know it. Then complete the chart.

This player
is shouting
because he is
angry about
how the game
is going. ▶

Rating Scale	**1** I have never seen this word before.	**2** I am not sure of the word's meaning.	**3** I know this word and can teach the word's meaning to someone else.

Key Words	Check Understanding	Deepen Understanding
❶ angry (**āng**-rē) *adjective* **Rating:** 1 2 3	When you feel **angry**, you are mad about something. Yes No	How do you help yourself feel better after you get angry? _____ _____ _____ _____
❷ different (**di**-fur-rent) *adjective* **Rating:** 1 2 3	Friends can have **different** ideas and still like each other. Yes No	Name two different languages. _____ _____ _____
❸ friendship (**frend**-ship) *noun* **Rating:** 1 2 3	**Friendship** develops when people like each other. Yes No	Name one important thing in a friendship. _____ _____ _____

Name _____

▲ This **group** is made of many **different** people who are all friends.

Key Words	Check Understanding	Deepen Understanding
❹ **group** (groop) *noun* **Rating:** 1 2 3	You can play music in more than one **group**. Yes No	Describe a group that you belong to. _____ _____ _____ _____
❺ **hoped** (hōpt) *verb* **Rating:** 1 2 3	Many people have **hoped** for world peace. Yes No	Describe something you have hoped for. _____ _____ _____ _____

B. Use at least two of the Key Vocabulary words. Tell about a time when you learned something from someone from a different group.

_____

_____

_____

Name _____

Plan and Write

1. Think about a time when you did something fun with a friend. What did you do? Where did you do it? How did you feel? Use the chart to answer the questions.

What We Did	Where	My Feelings

2. Write a title.

_____

3. Tell the **names** of your friends in the first sentence.

4. Tell what you did. Use the **past tense**. Tell how you felt. Use **feeling words**.

_____

_____

_____

_____

_____

_____

_____

_____

Check Your Work

▶ Capitalization and Focus

Read the memory story. Fix capital letters as needed. Take out any sentences that are not about the memory. Mark your changes. Then write the story correctly.

A Green Day with Kwami

by Declan O'Carroll

One day Kwami asked me to lunch at his house. Mrs. jones cooked a special meal. I was surprised when i saw the plate. It had green mashed potatoes, green beans, and green eggs! My sister Zeena is a good cook. We ate the green food. It looked funny but tasted good! Then kwami and i went downtown to the St. patrick's Day parade. Everyone wore green. It was a green day!

_____

_____

_____

_____

_____

_____

_____

_____

_____

_____

_____

_____

_____

Mind Map

Use the mind map to show how people celebrate. As you read the selections in this unit, add new ideas you learn about the ways people celebrate around the world.

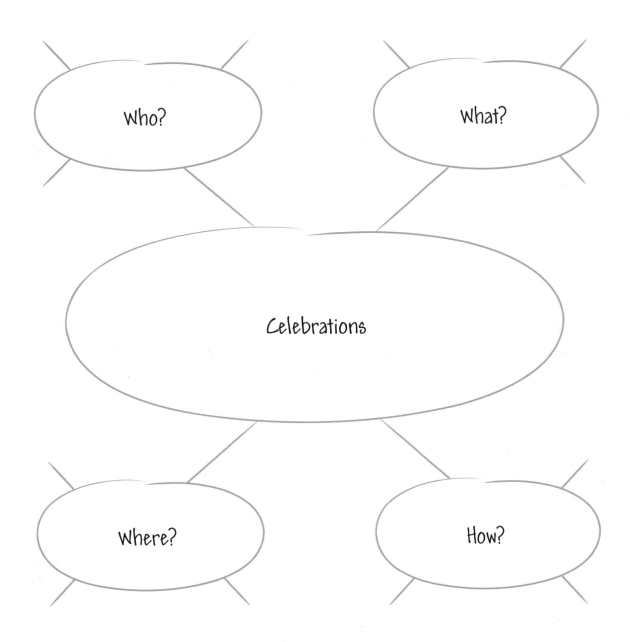

How Does He Dance?

▶ **Language: Ask and Answer Questions**
▶ **Grammar: Adverbs**

Look at each picture. Answer the question. Use an adverb from the box.

up	back	high	slowly	forward	now

1.

Where does Matt stretch?

Matt stretches ____up____ .

2.

Where does Matt reach?

He reaches _____ .

3.

How does Matt bend?

Matt bends _____ .

4.

Can Matt go back?

No, Matt can't go _____ .

5.

Can Matt jump?

Yes, Matt can jump _____ .

6.

When can he dance?

He can dance _____ .

What Are They Doing?

▶ **Grammar: Present Progressive Verbs**

These verbs tell what is happening now.

The girls **are celebrating** their culture.
They **are standing** in line.
The powwow **is starting** soon.

Complete each sentence. Tell what the people are doing. Use verbs from the box.

are moving	is stepping	are enjoying	are playing
is singing	are sitting	is hopping	is listening

1. The dancer _____is stepping_____ quickly.

2. His feet _____ forward.

3. He _____ up and down.

4. He _____ to the music.

5. The children _____ in a circle.

6. They _____ the drums.

7. One boy _____ a song.

8. The children _____ the music.

Language Development

Dancers Around the World

▶ **Vocabulary: Country Words**
▶ **Language: Describe People**

A. Look at each picture. Complete the sentences. Use words from the box.

Scotland	Scottish	Cambodia	Cambodian

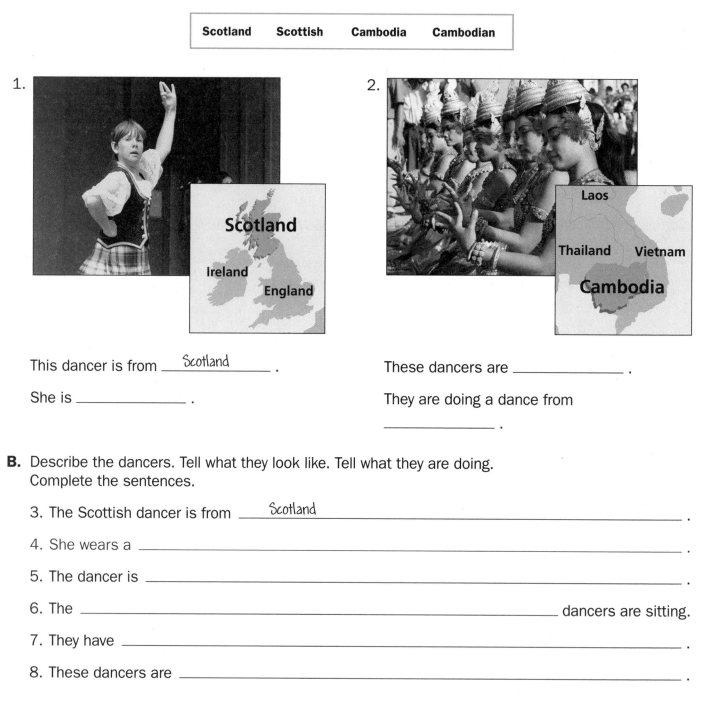

1.

This dancer is from ____Scotland____ .

She is _____ .

2.

These dancers are _____ .

They are doing a dance from

_____ .

B. Describe the dancers. Tell what they look like. Tell what they are doing.
Complete the sentences.

3. The Scottish dancer is from ____Scotland_____ .

4. She wears a _____ .

5. The dancer is _____ .

6. The _____ dancers are sitting.

7. They have _____ .

8. These dancers are _____ .

We Like to Dance!

▶ **Grammar: Phrases with *Like To* and *Want To***

Use a verb to complete a phrase with *like to* or *want to*.

like to	+	verb

They **like to dance** together.

She **likes to step** to the music.

want to	+	verb

They **want to learn** more steps.

He **wants to teach** people.

Add an -s when you use he, she, or it.

Complete the sentences for each picture. Use *like to* or *want to*.

1.

The students ____like to____ leap.

They _____ perform for the Russian ballet.

2.

The boy _____ spin.

He _____ dance fast.

3.

The boys _____ celebrate the Chinese New Year.

They _____ carry the dragon costume.

4.

The dancer from India _____ share a story.

She _____ show it with her dance.

Classify Information

► **Sum It Up**

A. Think about the kind of dancing you like to do. Fill in the concept map. Tell
who you dance with, why you dance, where you dance, and how you dance.

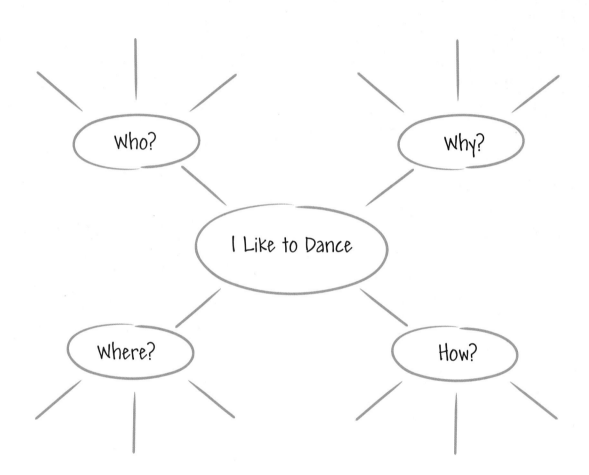

B. Write sentences to tell about the way you like to dance. Use words from
your concept map in your sentences.

_____

_____

_____

High Frequency Words, Part 1

A. Read each word. Then write it.

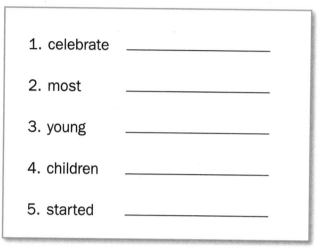

1. celebrate   _____

2. most   _____

3. young   _____

4. children   _____

5. started   _____

B. Write the answer to each question. Find the new words in the box. Write the words on the lines.

6. This word ends in **e**.

_____ celebrate _____

7. These 2 words have **st**.

_____   _____

8. This word is the opposite of **old**.

_____

9. This word begins with **ch**.

_____

10. This word is the opposite of **ended**.

_____

High Frequency Words, Part 2

A. Read each word. Then write it.

1. beginning _____

2. change _____

3. another _____

4. only _____

5. following _____

B. Read each sentence. Find the new words in the box. Write the words on the lines.

6. These 2 words end with **ing**.

    _____following_____   _____

7. This word ends with **e**.

    _____

8. This word has the word **other** in it.

    _____

9. Which word has 4 letters?

    _____

10. This word starts with **f**.

    _____

Verbs with -*ing*

A. Read each sentence. Change the word in dark type to tell what is happening right now.

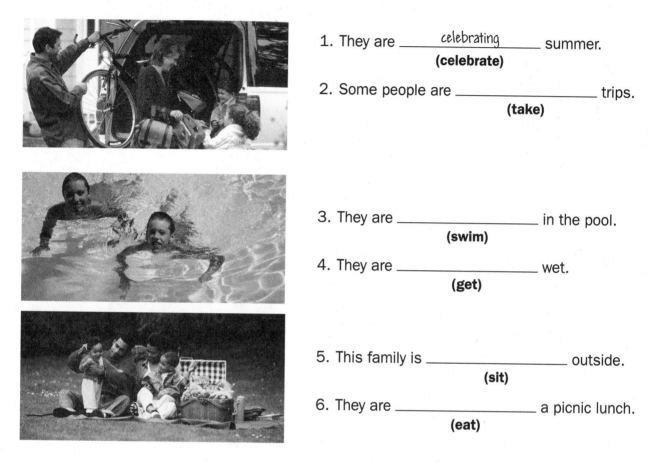

1. They are ___celebrating___ summer.
   (celebrate)

2. Some people are _____ trips.
   (take)

3. They are _____ in the pool.
   (swim)

4. They are _____ wet.
   (get)

5. This family is _____ outside.
   (sit)

6. They are _____ a picnic lunch.
   (eat)

B. Now read the story. Circle the words with -*ing*. Write each word in the chart one time. Then write the root word.

Our School Fair

Our school fair is (beginning) at 2 p.m. We are taking all the games outside. Suddenly, it is raining and we are beginning to get very wet. Most of us are rushing inside. Now we are waiting for the rain to stop. Yes. The sun is shining again. The fair can begin on time.

Word with -*ing*	Root Word
7. beginning	begin
8. _____	_____
9. _____	_____
10. _____	_____
11. _____	_____
12. _____	_____

Name _____

Build Reading Fluency

▶ **Phrasing**

A. When you read, pause between groups of words that go together.

They are greeting / the Chinese dragon, / which brings good luck. //
People dance / to celebrate an important day / in the family. //

B. Listen to the story. When you hear a short pause, write a / .
When you hear a long pause, write //.

Example: This bride / is having fun at her wedding. //

Dance to Celebrate

People dance to celebrate a holiday. These people are beginning the Chinese

New Year with a dance. They are greeting the Chinese dragon, which brings

good luck. Nine men inside the costume are lifting the dragon with long poles.

Only one man is beating a drum. He is following the dragon.

People dance to celebrate an important day in the family. This bride is

having fun at her wedding. Three young men are lifting her in her seat while

her husband watches. The family is dancing around them. They are smiling and

clapping.

C. Now read the story to a partner. Read groups of words together. Make a
short pause when you see a /. Make a long pause when you see a //.

Learn Key Vocabulary

Name _____

Kite Festival: Key Vocabulary

A. Study each word. Circle a number to rate how well you know it. Then complete the chart.

Rating Scale	**1** I have never seen this word before.	**2** I am not sure of the word's meaning.	**3** I know this word and can teach the word's meaning to someone else.

▲ **Colorful** kites fly **gracefully** through the air.

Key Words	Check Understanding	Deepen Understanding
❶ celebrate (se-luh-brāt) *verb* **Rating:** 1 2 3	Americans **celebrate** the Fourth of July. Yes No	How do you celebrate a birthday? _____ _____ _____
❷ colorful (cul-er-ful) *adjective* **Rating:** 1 2 3	Gray skies are **colorful**. Yes No	Which of your clothes are colorful? _____ _____ _____
❸ enjoy (en-joi) *verb* **Rating:** 1 2 3	Most people **enjoy** holidays. Yes No	Tell what you enjoy about one holiday. _____ _____ _____

Name _____

Teams **celebrate** the kite festival by flying a **colorful** kite. ▶

Key Words	Check Understanding	Deepen Understanding
❹ **gracefully** (grās-ful-lē) *adverb* **Rating:** 1 2 3	Ballet dancers move **gracefully**. Yes No	Describe something that moves gracefully. _____ _____ _____ _____
❺ **started** (stär-ted) *verb* **Rating:** 1 2 3	The day has not **started** yet. Yes No	Describe how one of your family parties started. _____ _____ _____ _____

B. Use at least two of the Key Vocabulary words. Describe what it would be like to watch the kite festival in Japan.

_____

_____

_____

Writing Project

Plan and Write

1. Choose a celebration. _____

2. What do you want to write about? Make a list of questions.

   A. How _____

   B. Where _____

   C. What _____

3. Use your questions to interview someone about the celebration. Write the answers.

   A. _____

   B. _____

   C. _____

4. Write a title.

5. Name the **celebration** and the **country** in the first sentence.

6. Write sentences. Tell what people **like to** do at the celebration.

_____

_____

_____

_____

_____

_____

_____

_____

_____

_____

_____

_____

_____

Check Your Work

▶ Capitalization and Details

Read the blog. Fix capital letters where they are needed. Take out any detail that does not go with the topic. Mark your changes. Then write the blog correctly.

Chinese Lunar New Year

Many people from china celebrate the Lunar New Year. we go to parades where people dress like lions and dragons. There are similar celebrations for the new year in other countries like vietnam. We also go to parades on memorial day and the fourth of July. this celebration is also special because families get together for a reunion dinner and eat special food. Chinese Lunar New Year is celebrated in different months. Sometimes it falls in january. Sometimes it is in february.

_____

_____

_____

_____

_____

_____

_____

_____

_____

_____

_____

_____

_____

_____

_____

Timed Reading Chart

Name _____

How many words did you read correctly for each
selection? Complete the chart to show your scores
for each day.

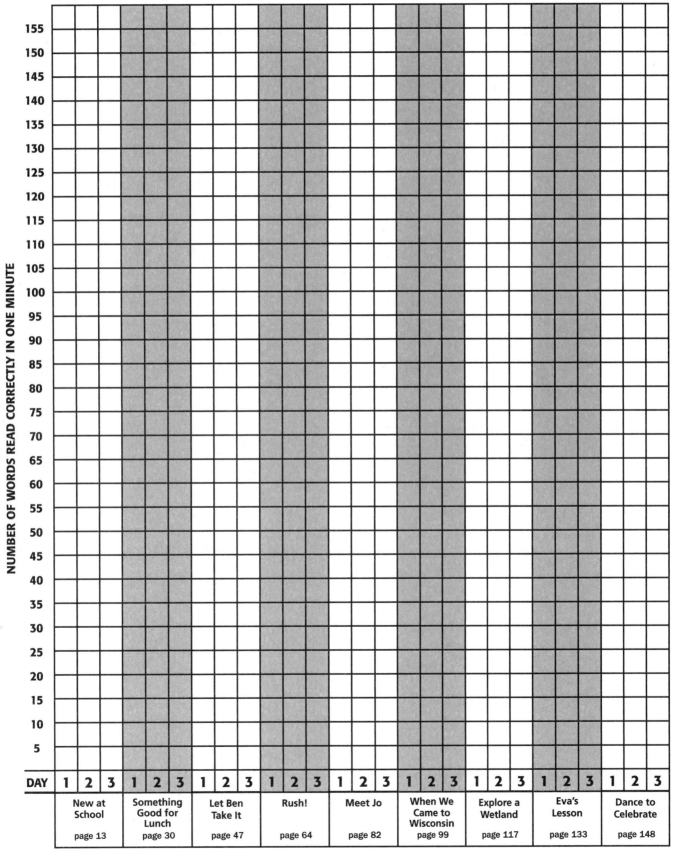

NUMBER OF WORDS READ CORRECTLY IN ONE MINUTE

DAY	1	2	3	1	2	3	1	2	3	1	2	3	1	2	3	1	2	3	1	2	3	1	2	3	1	2	3
	New at School page 13			Something Good for Lunch page 30			Let Ben Take It page 47			Rush! page 64			Meet Jo page 82			When We Came to Wisconsin page 99			Explore a Wetland page 117			Eva's Lesson page 133			Dance to Celebrate page 148		

Decodable Stories

Contents

Short *a* and Short *o*

A Bad Day!

This is not a good day!

Words with /ă/a; /ŏ/o		
am	class	lot
and	dad	mad
at	ham	mom
bad	has	not
bag	hot	sad
can	jog	stops
		tan
		van

High Frequency Words for Unit 1
home

Unit 1 Glad to Meet You!

2

I am at school at 8:00.

I am at lunch at 12:00. I have hot ham. I do not like ham. I am sad and mad.

2

7

I have a class at 8:15. I do not have my tan bag. My tan bag is at home.

I jog a lot in P.E. I am hot! I stop.

Mom is mad. Mom can not come. Dad can.

Dad stops the van. Dad has my tan bag.

Fold

4

5

Short *i*, Short *u*, *ch*, and *tch*

It is such a mess! Mom does not like it a bit. Jim just grins.

Catch, Mom!

Words with /ĭ/*i*; /ŭ/*u*; /ch/*ch*, tch

bag	fills	it	stuff
big	grabs	Jim	such
bit	grins	just	switch
bunch	hits	much	will
but	hunts	pop	
catch	in	rip	
fast	is	snack	

High Frequency Words for Units 1–2

open	then	there

Unit 2 Set the Table

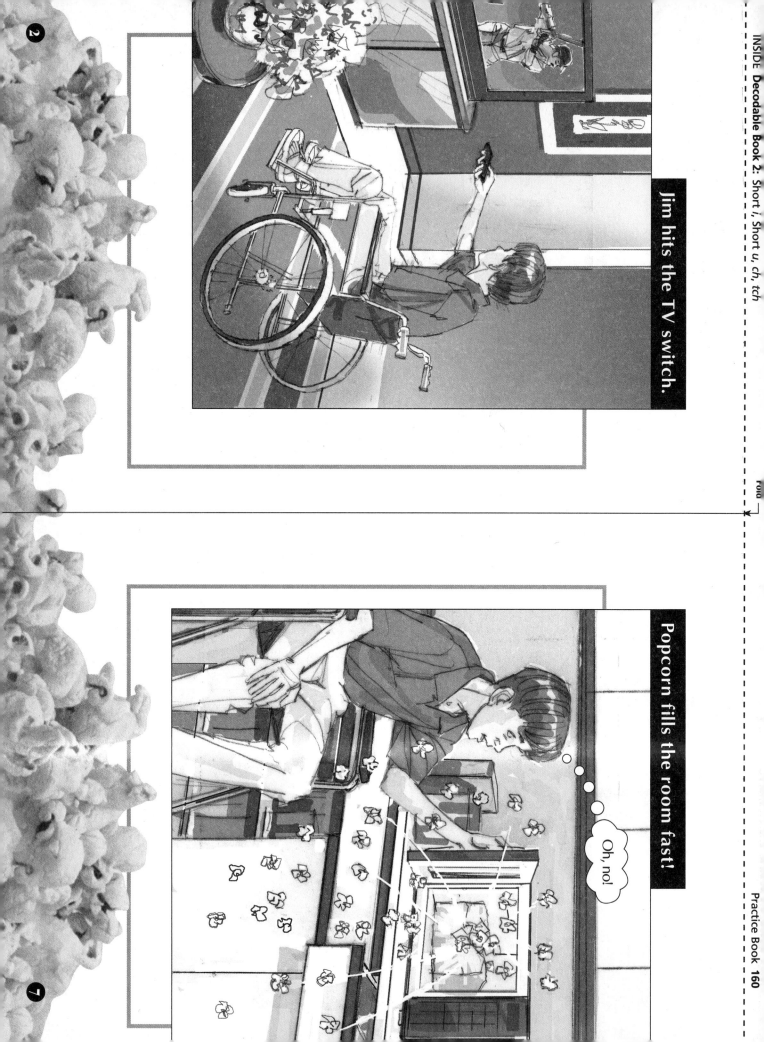

Jim hits the TV switch.

Popcorn fills the room fast!

Oh, no!

Then Jim hunts for a snack. There is just a bunch of old stuff, but Jim does spot a bag of . . .

Popcorn! It will pop fast.

Jim looks at his snack. Jim can spot a rip in the bag. Jim opens the microwave.

3

6

It will not take much time.

Jim grabs a bag. He does not spot a rip in the bag.

Jim can mix punch as it pops.

5

Short e, sh, ck, and Double Consonants

Fred at Work

At last, the day ends. Mom has one last job for Fred.

Zzzzzzz

Fred! Help me carry these bags.

Where is Fred? He is in bed! Zzzzzzz.

© NGSP & HB

Words with ĕ/e/; /sh/sh; /k/ck

bed	Fred	mess	stack
chest	fresh	net	trash
docks	gets	picks	when
ends	help	shop	yes

High Frequency Words for Units 1-3

| love | there | want |

Unit 3 On the Job

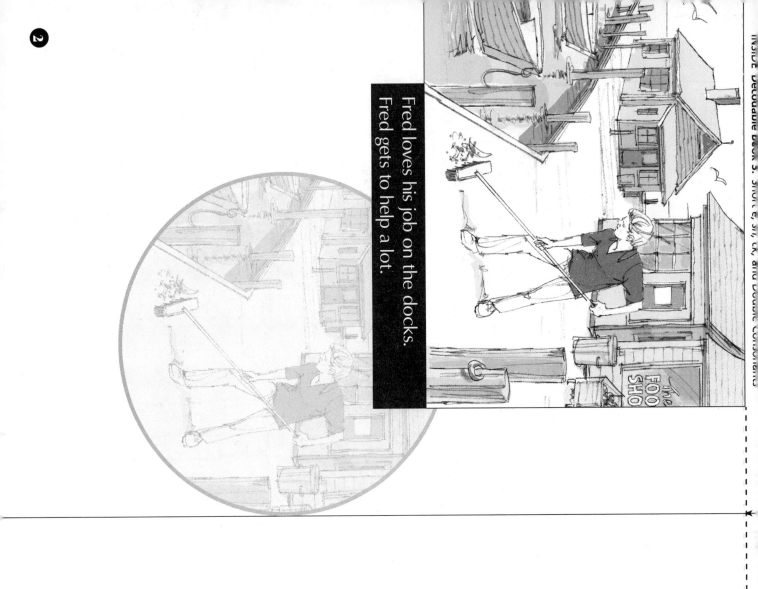

Fred loves his job on the docks.
Fred gets to help a lot.

Fred takes trash to a bin.

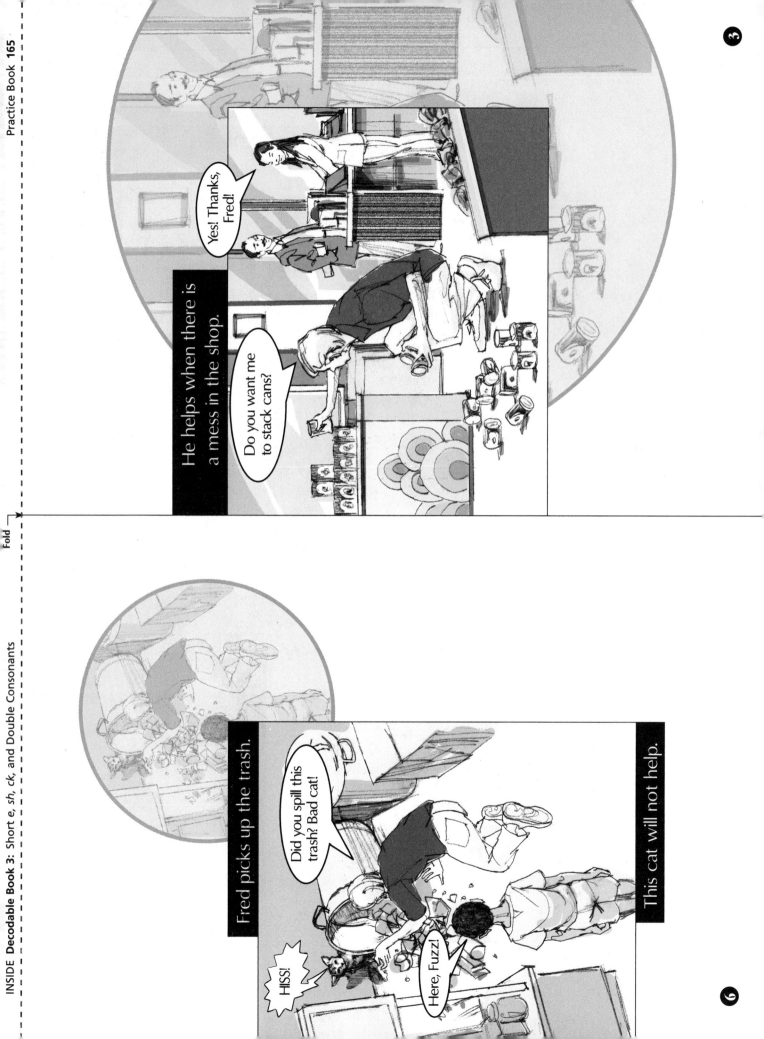

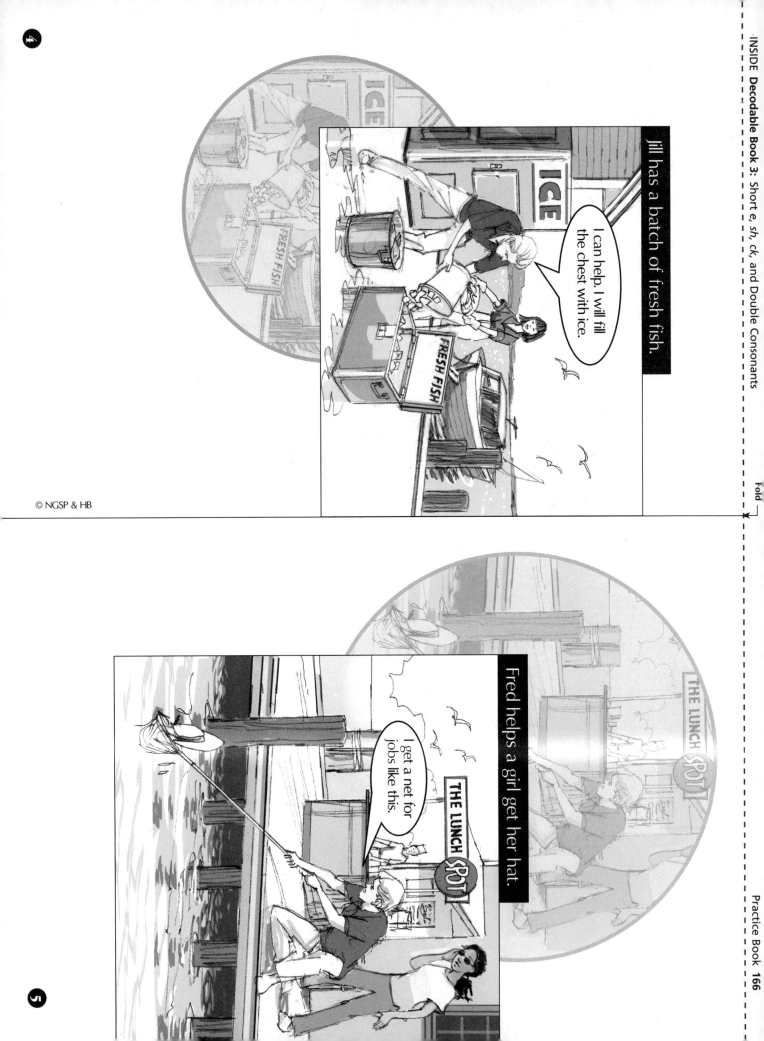

Jill has a batch of fresh fish.

I can help. I will fill the chest with ice.

Fred helps a girl get her hat.

I get a net for jobs like this.

Fold

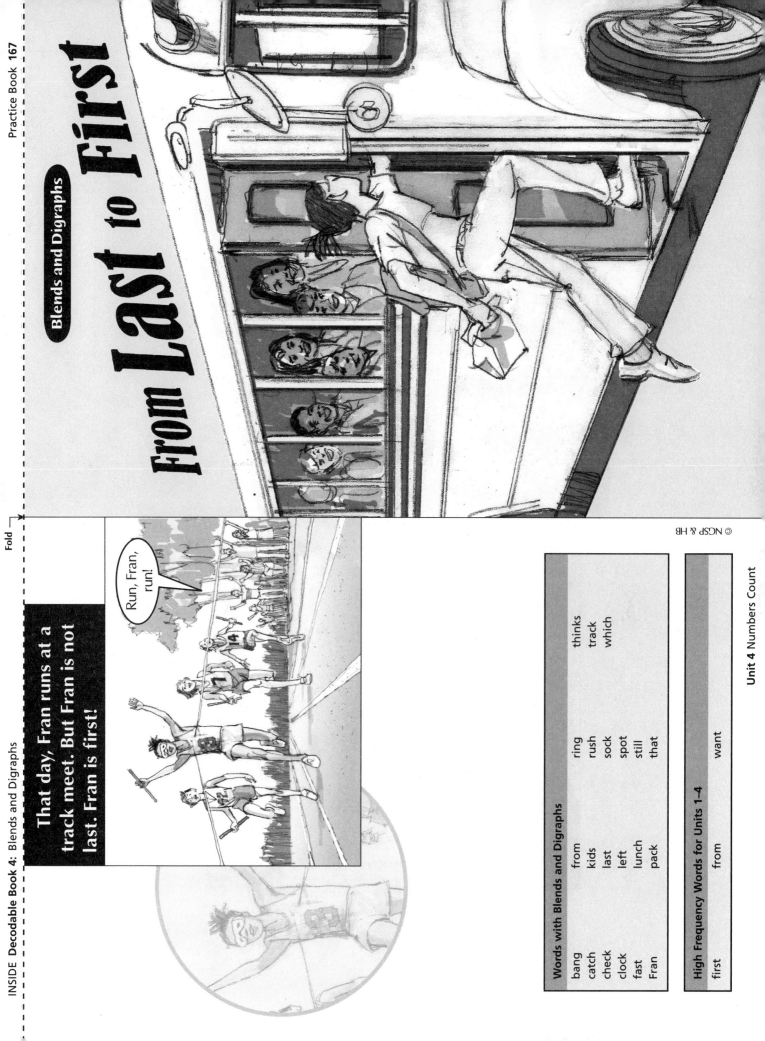

Blends and Digraphs

From *Last* to *First*

That day, Fran runs at a track meet. But Fran is not last. Fran is first!

Run, Fran, run!

Words with Blends and Digraphs

bang	from	ring	thinks
catch	kids	rush	track
check	last	sock	which
clock	left	spot	
fast	lunch	still	
Fran	pack	that	

High Frequency Words for Units 1–4

first	from	want

Unit 4 Numbers Count

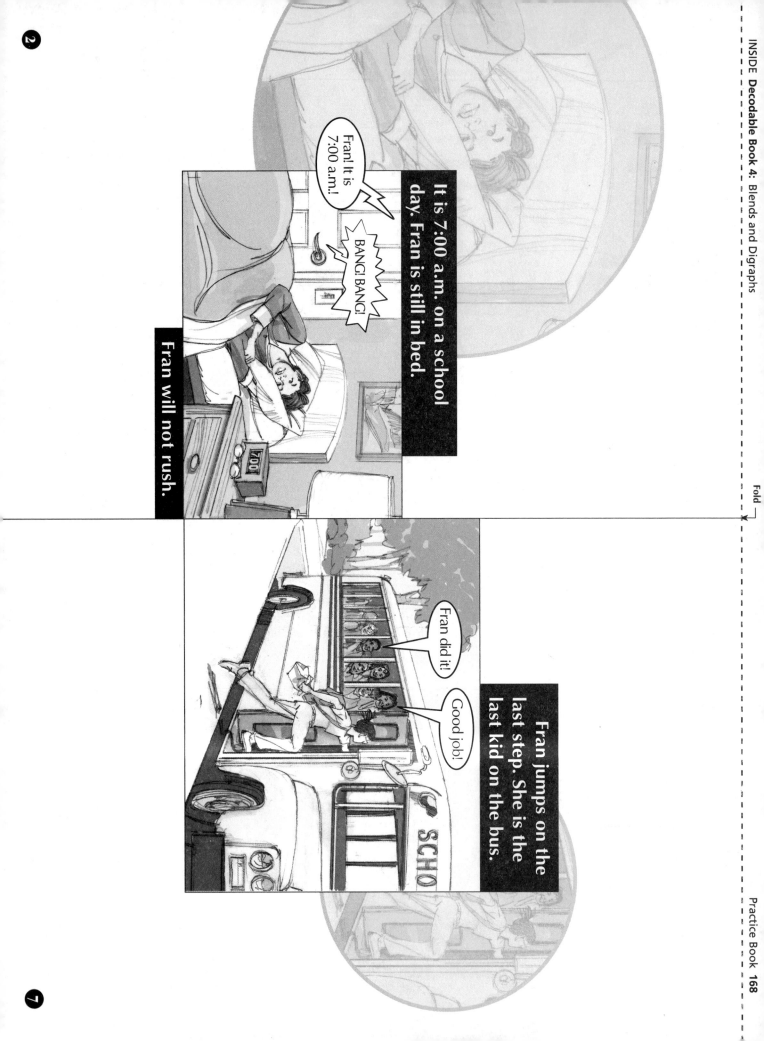

It is 7:00 a.m. on a school day. Fran is still in bed.

Fran! It is 7:00 a.m.!

BANG! BANG!

Fran will not rush.

Fran jumps on the last step. She is the last kid on the bus.

Good job!

Fran did it!

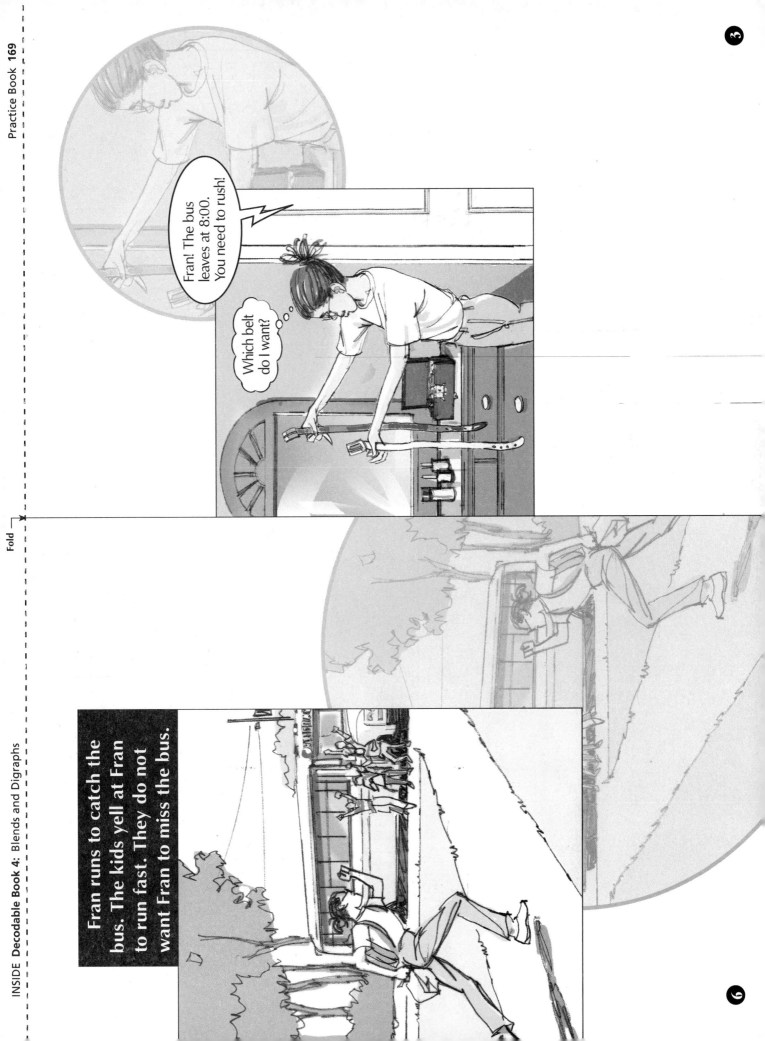

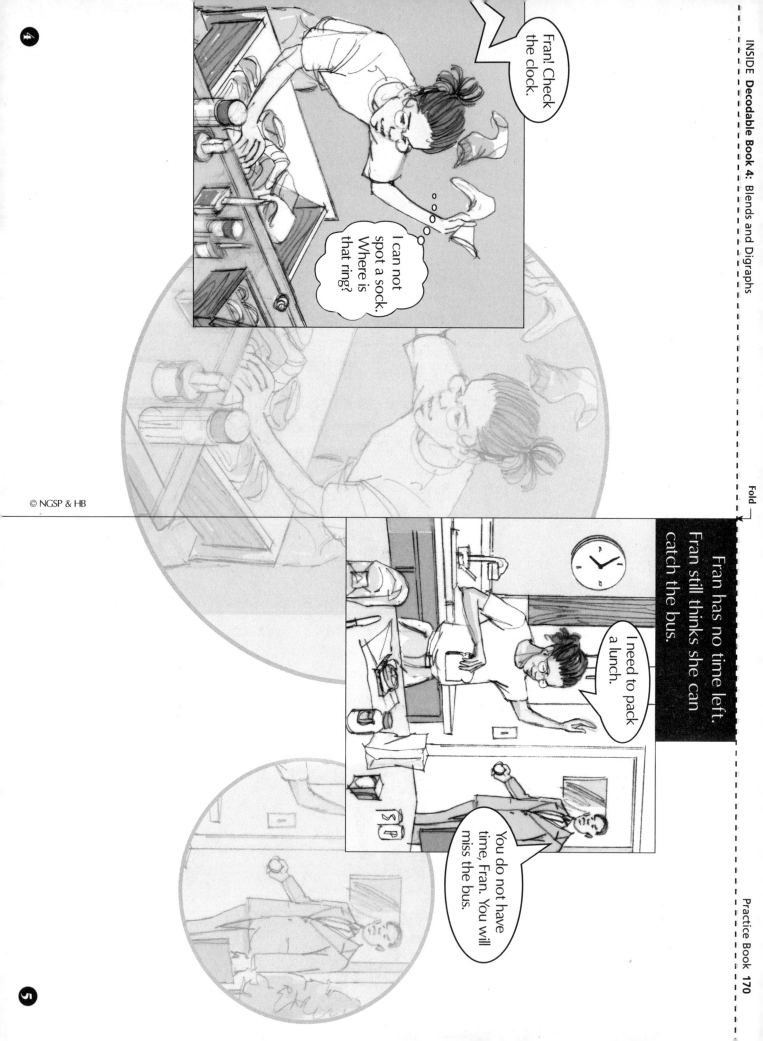

A City Food Festival

© NGSP & HB

Fold

We can't stop yet!

You go. I can't move. No more food festivals for me.

EXIT

Word Patterns and Multisyllabic Words

basket	happens	stand	crab
chips	hundreds	stands	sandwich
chopsticks	is	sum	has
dim	muffins	that	had
Ekram	napkin	this	
festival	Pedro	with	
fish	shish-ke-bob	pumpkin	

High Frequency Words for Units 1–5

all	first	new	something
city	love	next	there
enough	more	people	want
find	move	second	

Unit 5 City Sights

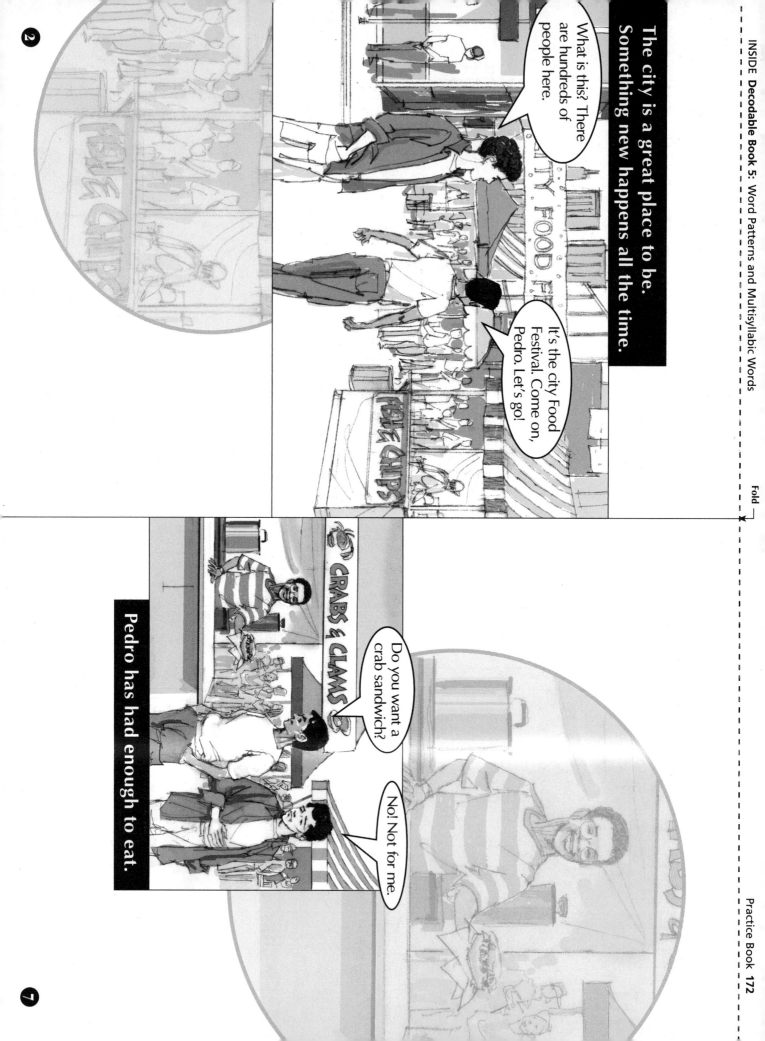

The city is a great place to be. Something new happens all the time.

What is this? There are hundreds of people here.

It's the city Food Festival. Come on, Pedro. Let's go!

Do you want a crab sandwich?

No! Not for me.

Pedro has had enough to eat.

2

7

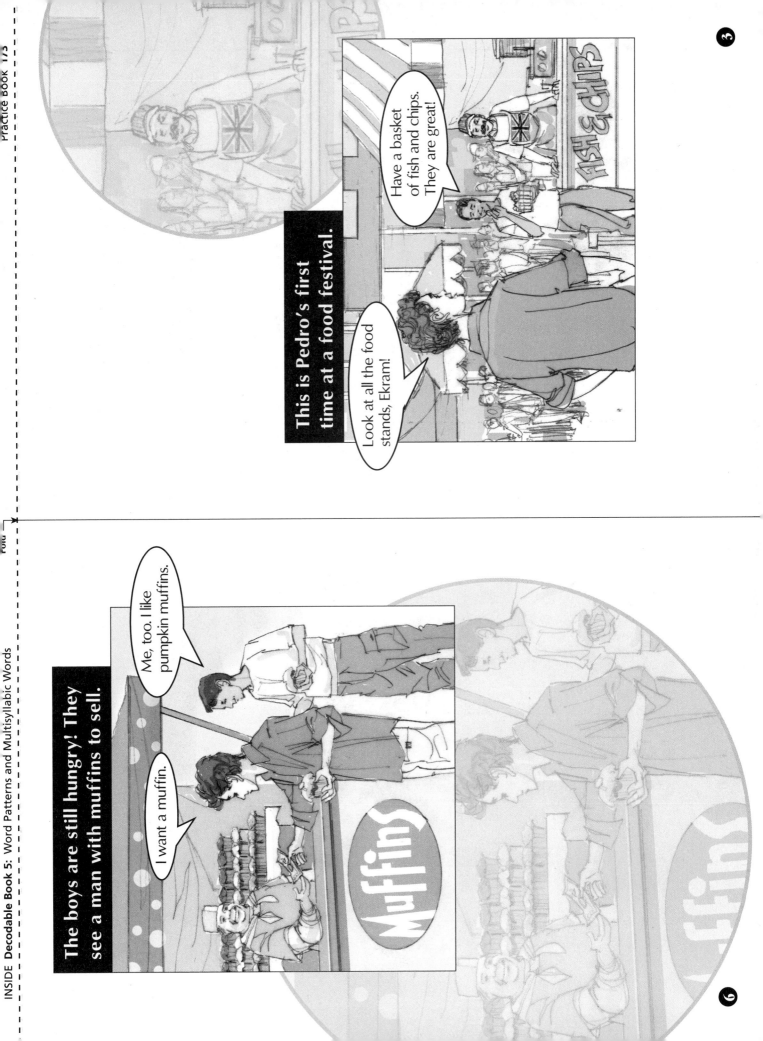

The boys smell lots of good food. Their second stop is a stand that sells Chinese food.

Do you like dim sum?

Yes, I do. I love to eat with chopsticks, too.

Next they find a stand that sells Greek food.

Look! Shish-ke-bob. It's lunch on a stick.

I need a napkin.

4

5

Long Vowels: *a, i, o, u*

At Home

INSIDE Decodable Book 6: Long Vowels: *a, i o, u*

Grandmother likes all the things we do for her. She even likes my brother's drums.

BANG!

CRASH!

Words with Long Vowels: *a, i, o, u*

cakes	hope	robe	tune
bake	like	smiles	use
fine	make	take	
home	notes	time	

High Frequency Words for Units 1–6

all	from	out	wants
down	her	together	
eat	our	something	

Unit 6 Welcome Home!

My grandmother is here from Japan. Our family is glad to see her. We hope she likes our home.

I like this food! The cake is good, too!

Soon it is time to eat. We use our best dishes for the food. We take out the best glasses. Then we sit down and eat together. Grandmother smiles and smiles.

It smells good!

We want to make Grandmother glad that she came to see us. So we think of special things to do for her. In Japan, Grandmother does not bake cakes. So I make her one.

My mother makes crab rolls for Grandmother.

We really like these. I hope she will, too.

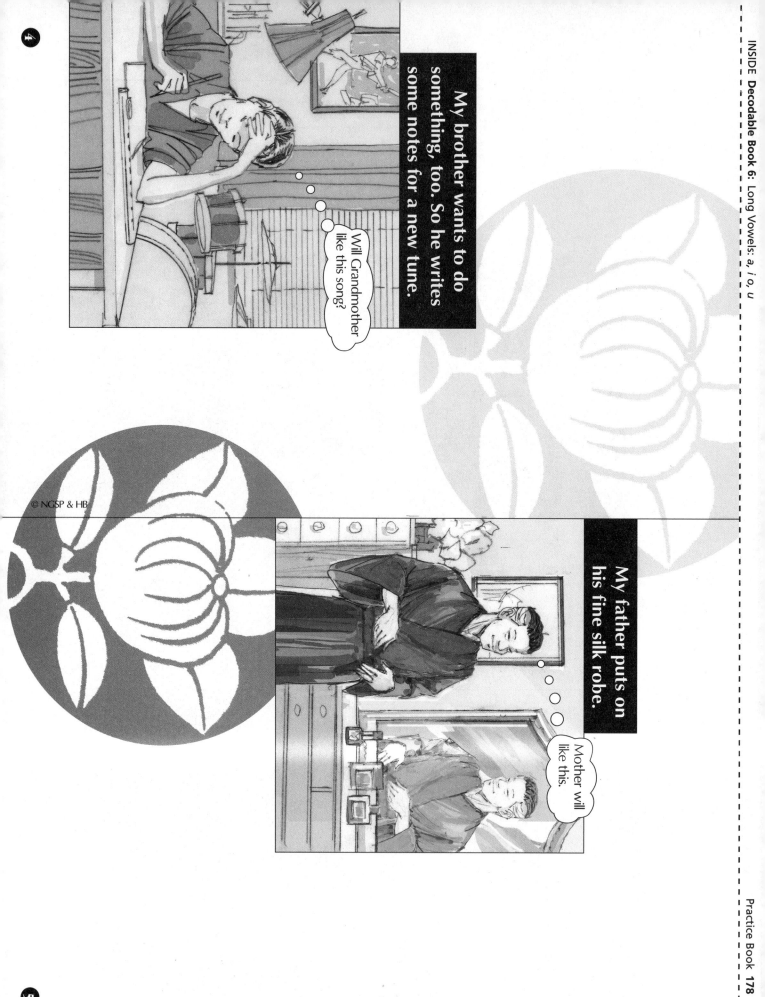

Long Vowels: *ai, ay; ee, ea; oa, ow* and Compound Words

On the River

It's the end of the day.

Well, we don't have any fish.

No, but we had a neat day, and it didn't rain!

© NGSP & HB

Words with Long Vowels: *ai, ay; ee, ea; oa, ow*

cattail	deep	neat	toad
croak	eats	rain	weekend
day	hears	show	year
daytime	near	sleep	

High Frequency Words for Units 1–7

always	place	something	there
animals	river	small	water
one			

Unit 7 Pack Your Bags!

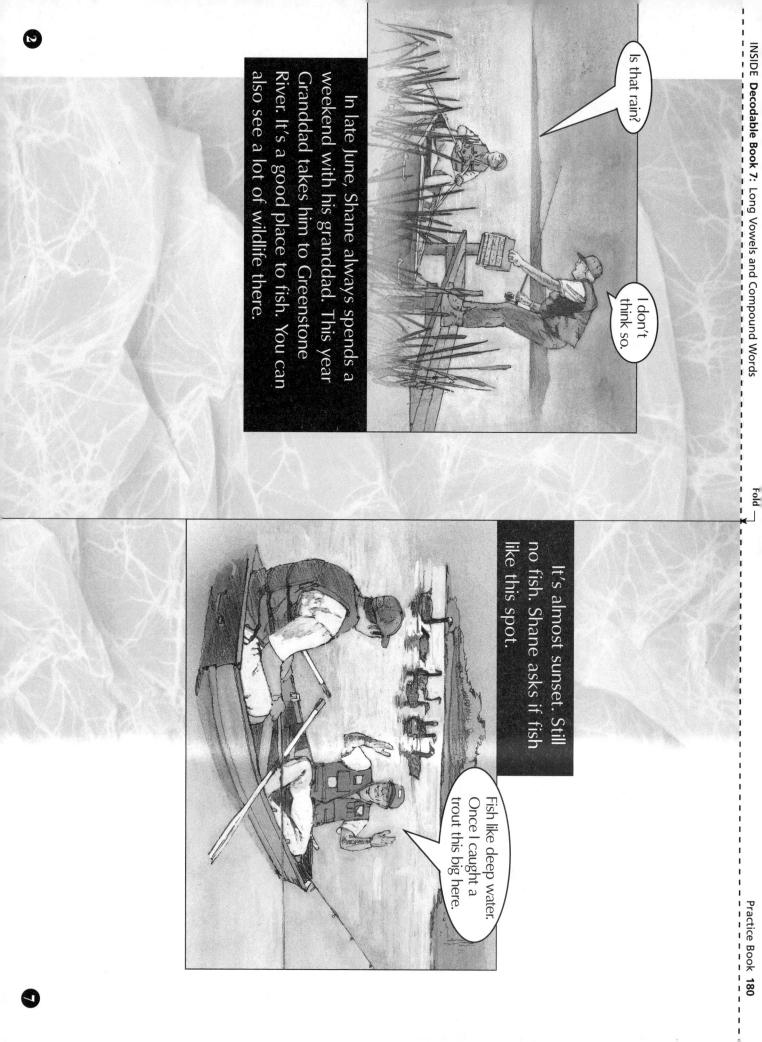

Is that rain?

I don't think so.

In late June, Shane always spends a weekend with his granddad. This year Granddad takes him to Greenstone River. It's a good place to fish. You can also see a lot of wildlife there.

It's almost sunset. Still no fish. Shane asks if fish like this spot.

Fish like deep water. Once I caught a trout this big here.

Fold

4

They wait for the fish to bite. While they wait, Shane sees something.

Look!

That's a bald eagle! It hunts for small animals that live by the water. It eats fish, too.

5

Shane hears something in the cattail plants.

Look at the toad!

That's a tree frog. Frogs can be hard to spot. They sleep in the daytime.

Hi, Duke! How are you? How is your new home?

Chen, do I need to tell you again? Your dog is just fine!

WOOF!

Words with Verb Ending -ed

hated	jogged	sailed	waited
hunted	played	stepped	

High Frequency Words for Units 1–8

about	animals	really	together
again	love	there	was
always	new	thought	were

Before I came here, Duke and I were always together. He waited for me after school. He was there to greet me when I stepped off the bus.

We love books. Let's find some books to read together.

Duke even liked to sit with me and look at books.

Verb Ending -ing

Celebrate the Past

Children are singing as we leave the fair. I look back, wondering if we really went into the past.

It's fun to celebrate the past this way!

Words with Verb Ending -ing		
beginning	joking	singing	thinking
dressing	pinning	slapping	throwing
eating	playing	taking	
getting	scrubbing	tasting	

High Frequency Words for Units 1–9		
another	come	really	want
celebrate	people	something	young
city			

Unit 9 Let's Celebrate!

My friends are taking me to a fair. It is like a trip back in time.

This seems like a city in old England.

A play is beginning, and the actors are speaking to me! They ask me to come on the stage and be the queen!